The Pocket Mentor for Game Audio

Want to work as an audio professional in the video games industry? Then this is the book for you. It provides all the essential information and guidance you need to understand the industry and get your foot on the ladder.

The book covers everything from the education you'll need, how to look for and apply for job opportunities and what to do once you land your first job. It also includes advice on what to do once you're in the role, with chapters covering best practices for sound designers, how to set goals for future career progression, as well as top tips from experts in the industry. It is written as a companion to the Game Audio Learning (GAL) website and invites the reader to visit GAL to access additional information that expands on the book's contents.

This book will be of great interest to all beginner and aspiring game audio professionals, as well as more experienced game audio professionals who are looking for new ways to approach their career planning.

The Pocket Mentors for Games Careers Series

The Pocket Mentors for Games Careers provide the essential information and guidance needed to get and keep a job in the modern games industry. They explain in simple, clear language exactly what a beginner needs to know about education requirements, finding job opportunities, applying for roles, and acing studio interviews. Readers will learn how to navigate studio hierarchies, transfer roles and companies, work overseas, and develop their skills.

The Pocket Mentor for Video Game Writers
Anna Megill

The Pocket Mentor for Video Game Testing
Harún Ali

The Pocket Mentor for Game Community Management
Carolin Wendt

The Pocket Mentor for Animators
Hollie Newsham

The Pocket Mentor for Game Audio
Greg Lester and Jonny Sands

For more information about this series, please visit: https://www.routledge.com/The-Pocket-Mentors-for-Games-Careers/book-series/PMGC

The Pocket Mentor for Game Audio

Greg Lester and Jonny Sands

CRC Press
Taylor & Francis Group
Boca Raton London New York

CRC Press is an imprint of the
Taylor & Francis Group, an **informa** business

Designed cover image: Greg Lester and Jonny Sands

First edition published 2025
by CRC Press
2385 NW Executive Center Drive, Suite 320, Boca Raton FL 33431

and by CRC Press
4 Park Square, Milton Park, Abingdon, Oxon, OX14 4RN

CRC Press is an imprint of Taylor & Francis Group, LLC

ISBN: 978-1-032-43787-3 (hbk)
ISBN: 978-1-032-43788-0 (pbk)
ISBN: 978-1-003-36885-4 (ebk)
ISBN: 978-1-003-50715-4 (eBook+)

DOI: 10.1201/9781003368854

Typeset in Times
by KnowledgeWorks Global Ltd.

Thank you to Mom, Dad and Phoebe, for their unwavering support; Jonny, without whom I could not have climbed this mountain; Lewis Thompson, to whom I owe most of my career; Sean Cooper, for taking a chance on me; David Fairfield, for being a friend and mentor; Jon Kelliher, for always being there to talk; the Soundcuts team, for helping me become a better sound designer every day; and the game audio community, and all *Airwigglers* – you inspire me on a daily basis!

– Greg

Thank you to my wonderful parents and brother Cameron, for their enthusiasm and encouragement; to Emile and Kate, who were there for me when I needed them most; and to Greg, for asking me to give feedback on a YouTube video back in 2018.

– Jonny

Contents

Acknowledgements

Our thanks to the following industry friends and colleagues, whose insights were invaluable in writing this book:

Adele Cutting, Ash Read, Ashton Mills, Ben Gallagher, Cai Jones, Calum Fox Forrest, Chris Jolley, David Fairfield, Giovane Webster, Jake Gaule, Jamie Baker, Jamie Lee, Jon Kelliher, Lewis Thompson, Mark Winter, Sarah Sherlock, Sean Cooper and Sergio Ronchetti.

Author Biographies

Greg Lester is a professional sound designer for video games who enjoys venturing beyond the medium on occasion in search of knowledge he can apply in his work. His passion for learning and teaching has granted him opportunities to teach at both undergraduate and postgraduate degree levels. Universities didn't quite satisfy his appetite for education and community, however, so with the help of Jonny Sands, he created the Game Audio Learning (GAL) website and co-founded Airwiggles with Lewis Thompson. His mission is to make game audio accessible to everyone.

Jonny Sands is a freelance guitarist, producer and co-creator of Game Audio Learning. He and Greg met at university and quickly bonded over a shared love of video games and electronic music. In 2018, Greg approached Jonny asking for feedback on a YouTube video examining the sound design of Cuphead, for what eventually became the GAL YouTube channel. Today, Jonny manages the behind-the-scenes admin for GAL and Airwiggles, working with Greg to achieve the vision of producing freely available educational material for all.

Intro
What's This Book About?

Hello and welcome! My name is Greg Lester – I'm a full-time professional in video game audio, and if you're reading this book, I imagine that you want to be as well. If so, you're in luck, as this book is written specifically for you! When I took my first steps into the world of game audio, I had no idea what to do or where to go, but with the help of some amazing people and a fair bit of luck, I managed to find my way into a full-time job and build myself the foundations of a stable career.

This book is the one I wish that I'd had when I was starting out. It's the product of all the mistakes I've made and the lessons I've learned, as well as the wisdom of friends and mentors who've made the journey into a game audio career in their own ways. It'll act as your travel guide, helping you figure out where you want to go and how to get there without burning out along the way. We'll discuss how to make the transition from game audio as a hobby to a career, the value of being a team player, and the importance of continuous learning and self-improvement. Exciting, no?

As you may have noticed, the primary focus of this book is on the 'soft skills' you need for a career in game audio rather than the technical details of DAWs and game engines. There are two reasons for this. First is that educational materials relating to game audio (or the games industry in general) tend to focus on technical knowledge over soft skills – knowing how to do the job is important, obviously, but so is being able to grow into your career in a healthy and sustainable manner. Second, is that the games industry is incredibly fast-moving, and the technical standards are perpetually changing. Since I can't just release a patch for a physically printed book, I want to focus on the things that will still be relevant 5, 10, 20 years from now (shoutout to anyone reading this in 2044!).

Technical knowledge is still important, of course, and there will be moments in this book where there's more that could be said about specific topics if I had more words. That's where *Game Audio Learning* comes in: A website I created with the help of my co-author Jonny, designed to be an accessible starting point for anyone looking to get into game audio, covering both technical and soft skills. Throughout this book, you'll see references to the *GAL* website – when you do, head to *gameaudiolearning.com/pocket-mentor* to access the landing page we've created just for this book, with additional resources and further reading for key topics.

The people who will get the most out of this book are the "doers." The games industry is a competitive place, and building a career in the space requires you to be committed to learning and taking action. That doesn't mean that you'll either land a job in 6 months or never make it, but it does mean that you'll need to put the effort in. Through this book, I'll help you avoid some of the pitfalls I encountered, and with a bit of luck, we'll see you build a successful career for yourself in an exciting and ever-changing industry!

With all that said, let's begin at the beginning, with some basic questions to orient ourselves…

Where Do
I Start?

1

How do I get into game audio?
Where do I even start?

The first time I found myself faced with these questions was at the start of my own journey into game audio. Since that day they've managed to find their way back to me again and again through my email inbox, the comment sections of my YouTube videos, DMs on social media or just directly into my ears from people I meet in person. I've thought about it a lot, researching and discussing with folks throughout the industry, trying to find the perfect answer. In the process I've created a YouTube channel, built two websites and now written this book, but the truth is: there is no single perfect answer that works universally – everyone's circumstances are so unique and varied that a catch-all solution is impossible. However, while I can't give you an easy answer to these questions, I can give you the tools to find the correct answers for *you*, and help you form a plan to get you on your way. To do that, we need to start with three different questions:

Where am I right now on my game audio journey?
Where do I want to go?
What route do I need to take to get there?

Once we know the answers to these questions, we can start to understand how you might begin to move forward and plan the next steps that you need to take to get where you want to go. This book and the *GAL* website will be your travel companions offering you tips and advice along the way.

IT'S A BIG WORLD OUT THERE

Imagine the world of game audio as a map in a video game, with different areas representing various fields and disciplines. Each area has its unique challenges and rewards; some areas are accessible almost immediately and

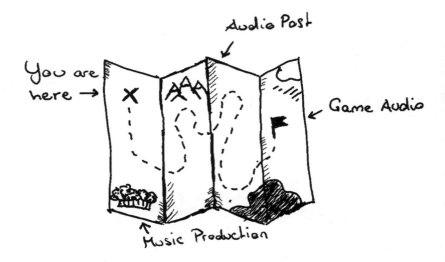

FIGURE 1.1   The world of game audio is itself part of a much larger world of general audio.

some require you to have more experience or skills before you can even enter. If we zoom out, however, we can see that the realm of game audio is in fact part of the even bigger world of general audio, containing areas like film, TV, live sound, recording, post-production and many, many more. There's a big overlap between game audio and the neighbouring areas, and the borders can often become blurry (Figure 1.1).

Chances are that right now, you are somewhere in the larger world of general audio trying to navigate towards game audio. The journey may seem simple on paper, but it's important to take a second and orient yourself before you set off, identifying where you are and what skills you have. We're going to spend some time figuring this out together, identifying exactly where you want to go and then plotting a route to get you there. What this route looks like will depend on the type of person you are, the life you want to lead and the ambitions you have. Your path through the map will be shaped by the people you meet, the things you do and the challenges you face along the way.

Finally, we'll take a closer look at *why* you want to go there in the first place – the driving force behind your journey. With all that done, we'll have an answer to that original question of "Where do I start?" and be able to create a plan of action, with a "main quest" to follow and a list of skills to level up in order to have the best chance of getting to where you want to be.

WHERE AM I RIGHT NOW?

I asked myself this question when I was in my first year of university, studying music production with the aim of becoming a DJ and solo artist. That path, I had begun to realise, just wasn't for me. My passion for games had grown stronger during my time away from home, as they helped me stay in touch with my friends. When I found out that working in game audio was a viable career path, I knew I needed to change my trajectory towards it.

That same year, five days before my 18th birthday, I got a phone call from my dad which flipped my entire world upside down. My mum had suffered a severe stroke and was walking on a tightrope between life and death. When she went into emergency surgery, the chances were slim, but against all odds she pulled through. After months in hospital, she had made an incredible recovery, but life would never be the same. Not only was she my rock and fierce loving mother, but she had also been the main earner of our household. The stroke had rendered her unable to work, and my dad had become her full-time carer. Thankfully, we had enough savings to cover my rent until I finished university, but with this change in our financial situation, I knew it was vital for me to become financially independent as soon as possible.

At the time I was living in England, having moved over to study music production at university. My parents had remained in Austria where I was born and raised. Moving back was not an option for me; there were no opportunities near my hometown, and I knew that if I went home, I wouldn't be able to afford to come back again. My goal became clear: get a job in game audio by the time I graduate, two years from now.

The reason I'm telling you all of this is to give you context, because context matters. Each person has a unique set of circumstances which have led them to their current location on the map. These include things like:

- Your geographic location – where do you live, and are there any industry connections nearby?
- Your knowledge and experience – are you a complete beginner or do you have existing relevant skills? Have you worked in the industry or a similar discipline before?
- Your education – what's your highest level of qualification?
- Your financial situation – do you have money saved? How much do you need to earn in order to support yourself?
- Your wellbeing – how is your mental and physical health?
- Your time and responsibilities – what existing commitments do you have (rent, family, etc.)? How much free time do you have to dedicate to learning something new?

These circumstances are determined by the things you've done, the decisions you've made and, of course, a healthy amount of random chance. You may be familiar with the gaming term RNG (short for "Random Number Generator"), used to describe anything beyond the player's control – the loot you receive when you open a chest, the cards you draw from a shuffled deck, that sort of thing. As players we are at the mercy of RNG; sometimes we get lucky and sometimes we don't. Similarly, in the real world, there are a lot of things that are completely out of our control – where you were born, what the weather will be like on your birthday, how tall you are, and so on. While random chance can make life harder, it's important to focus on the things that you can control; prepare, practise and improve, so that when opportunities arise then you'll be able to jump on them.

My circumstances at the time I made the pivot to game audio were defined by the things below:

- My geographic location – Guildford, England (a gamedev hub).
- My knowledge and experience – music composition and production, audio editing and some basic recording techniques; no game industry-specific experience.
- My education – completed a music production diploma; currently enrolled at university on a music production degree.
- My financial situation – enough savings to cover rent until I finish university (two years); two part-time jobs to cover necessities like food and bills, as well as essential tools for audio.
- My wellbeing – highly motivated and determined, but a little fragile due to stress from recent events in my family; physically healthy, with no injuries or issues that could impact my journey.
- My time and responsibilities – my degree course, my two part-time jobs and my relationship with my partner.

Considering our world map of audio, I found myself in the realm of music and the technical/production area within that. With a better understanding of my position (and a two-year time limit), I was ready to start figuring out where I wanted to go.

Task – You Are Here

Take some time to reflect on your current situation and answer the questions as I've done. Consider where you are now, and how your circumstances relate to a potential career in game audio. What knowledge and skills do you currently have, and what are the factors that might affect your ability to learn new things and find the time to work on developing yourself?

WHERE DO I WANT TO GO?

When I first decided to pivot towards game audio, I had no idea about all of the different career paths and job opportunities that were out there. To keep with our metaphor of a world map, I could only see a very small portion of the world; the rest was shrouded in fog. With so little visible to me, I jumped into the one area I could see: music composition for games.

> When I was younger, I knew I was creative, but I didn't know how that paired up with the games industry.
>
> *David Fairfield*

I had a background in music production, but I knew very little about how it related to game audio, so I decided to just dive in and immerse myself in all the information I could find. I started reading books, articles, blog posts and interviews, watching online talks and videos. One of the most influential resources that I stumbled across was a Game Developers Conference (GDC) talk by the composer Mick Gordon on how he created the soundtrack for DOOM (2016). The things he said and showcased in those 60 minutes dramatically changed my trajectory and had a lasting impact on my career.

In his talk, Mick explained how he used various guitar pedals and pieces of outboard gear to create four unique processing chains. These were all routed into his Digital Audio Workstation (DAW), allowing him to send audio through them and record the outputs. He sent sine waves through these chains which became distorted and mangled by all the processing into crazy and interesting sounds, that he then chopped up and used as the foundational elements of the soundtrack. He nicknamed his creation the "Doom Instrument."

While the concept of sound design wasn't completely new to me, my experience had been primarily with conventional synthesisers, and my initial experiments with composition for games had focused heavily on orchestral scores. Seeing and hearing the innovation and creativity that Mick brought to this project left me in awe and opened my eyes to a whole new world. It dawned on me that sound design was not just a tool for music composition, and the fog on the map receded to reveal sound design for games.

Mick's mantra throughout the talk was "change the process, change the outcome." I took this to heart and saved up some money to buy a small portable recorder. I started collecting sounds wherever I went, which transformed the way that I listened to the world around me and fundamentally changed my relationship with sound. It got me thinking about the creative potential that could be unlocked with the right approach, and I subsequently became fascinated with sound design. I began to slowly move away from music as I focused all of my time on this newly ignited passion. My direction had changed, and I had chosen the path into sound design.

Your dreams can change throughout your life, and you should be open to that.

Jon Kelliher

Your own journey through game audio will likely have a lot of twists and turns along the way; your priorities will change throughout your life, as mine did in that moment watching Mick's GDC talk. This is perfectly normal and something to be embraced. While it might make committing to a path a scary prospect, remember that just as what you want can change, so can the route you take. You can always pivot and adjust course, but without a direction you will get lost.

In fact, the clearer and more specific a direction you can give yourself in the moment, the better, as you'll be able to make the most of your time by choosing the most efficient path and making the right decisions along the way. Even within the job role of sound designer, details like the genre of game you work on, the size of the project (AAA vs indie), or the location of the workplace (in-office or remote work) can have a profound effect on how best to approach your journey, so even if it's not forever, having a clear goal for the present is valuable.

Task – What Matters to Me?

To help identify a goal, ask yourself some of the following questions:

- Do you enjoy having ownership over your own time, or prefer a steady routine?
- Do you like wearing many different hats, or having one or two areas of specialisation?
- Do you enjoy working in large teams with specialised roles, or small groups with more generalist, wide-reaching roles?
- Do you prefer to work with people in an office, or independently from home?
- Do you like working on bigger long-term projects for multiple years, or shorter ones that last a few weeks or months?
- Is progression within the same job role important to you, or do you like to change things up from time to time?

Careers in game audio can come in many different forms, so the more you can find out about yourself – your interests, talents, likes, dislikes, wants and needs – the easier it is to find a place in the industry that best suits you as a person, and in which you can grow and thrive. You can find out more about the various career paths available in the game audio industry on the *GAL* website.

By knowing where you want to go, you'll be able to "position" yourself in a way that gives you the best chance of building a career that aligns with the life you want to lead. Positioning means understanding the kind of person that an employer is looking for, or the kind of person that is needed for a specific role, and tailoring your approach to match. This can mean things like ensuring that your demo reel contains material relevant to the type of projects you're interested in working on, or networking and making friends in the industry spaces where you'd like to work. It's not possible to be all things to all people, but by knowing where you want to be, you can identify what the people in that area are looking for and focus on those traits and skills.

HOW DO I GET THERE?

After spending some time thinking about *where* you might want to go, it's time to figure out the route you'll take to get there. When I made the pivot towards sound design, I was venturing into completely new and unknown territory; I knew where I wanted to go, but I didn't know how to navigate the space between me and my goal. I needed an action plan: a roadmap, something that I could follow to help me stay focused, navigate obstacles and keep me on the right path.

In order to become a sound designer, I needed to acquire the knowledge and skills expected of a sound designer and be able to prove to others that I had them. I had no idea what that knowledge and those skills were, so the first step was to find out. I started with an extensive Google search for junior/associate/graduate sound design job openings and wrote down all of the required skills and criteria that they asked for. I compiled a list of the common skills and requirements that showed up and brainstormed how I could most effectively learn them.

Through my research, it became clear that it was absolutely essential to have a demo reel; without one, you wouldn't even be considered for most jobs. A lot of them also valued previous hands-on experience, but how do you get experience without a job, when you still need to learn the fundamentals? The answer was obvious: I had to become a sound designer. I needed to do the things a sound designer does, to simulate the work and try to make it as close to the real thing as possible, if not find ways to do it for real right now. I needed to acquire the skills, gain the knowledge and build my network.

Ultimately, you have to learn by doing.

Lewis Thompson

My plan was to convince my lecturers to let me change as many of my university assignments as possible to something game audio-related. At the same time, I would read and watch any game audio-related material I could find, and try to find work on smaller indie projects or at game jams to get experience working with people from other disciplines and provide material for my demo reel. With some luck, I might even be able to ship a small title and get my first credit. Lastly, I needed to meet people in the industry – or on the same path towards it as me – and start making friends and building a network. That would allow me to gain more insight into the job and the wider industry and improve my chances of finding opportunities.

The plan paid off, and my lecturers approved a new set of assignments, including ones where I would have to create a musical platformer game from scratch, build a fully-fledged sound library and replace the audio of a small demo game. These tasks would allow me to actively practise and acquire the skills I needed to build a career in game audio, with deadlines and lecturers to hold me accountable mimicking the external pressure that would be present in a professional setting. Even if you don't choose to study game audio or a similar subject at university, having an external pressure to hold you account-able can be an effective tool, ensuring that you get things done. We'll talk about education and accountability more later on in this book.

It's important to remember that each of our paths to our desired destinations are unique – some people reach their destination after a very short time, whereas for others it can take years to get where they want to be. Understanding this won't make the disappointment of getting rejected from a job any easier, but it might just prevent you from giving up when the going gets tough.

WHY DO I WANT TO GO THERE?

It might seem a strange question to ask after all of this thinking about goals and plans, but it's important to understand what it is that motivates us. While I was at university, I worked two different jobs to sustain myself. One was at the student union's café which was relatively relaxed, especially in the mornings where I mainly made coffee and organised the store room; the second was working in a fast-food restaurant in the food court of a huge shopping mall.

My shifts were usually on weekends, when it was busiest. Each till had two people working behind it – one taking orders, one fetching food and drinks from the kitchen – and people would queue ten-deep in front of you. Saturdays in particular were a whole other level of carnage, and the cacophony of machines beeping, managers barking instructions and customers grumbling was overwhelming. I remember going into the tiny, hot and stuffy break room, taking off my grey cap, peeling the thin brown hair net from my sweaty head and with a deep sigh sinking into the chair and closing my eyes. I would do everything in my power not to have to do this kind of work after university, I thought to myself.

It wasn't all bad, of course. In this line of work, you're exposed to a wide variety of different people from all walks of life. It forced me to get comfortable talking to complete strangers all day long and taught me the importance of teamwork and morale – lessons we'll talk about later in this book. Similar to those I took from my time working in fast food, we can take away valuable lessons from all kinds of situations and challenges in our lives and use them to our advantage.

Not wanting to do something or end up somewhere can be an incredibly strong source of motivation. While doing research for this book, I talked to multiple people who'd had terrible previous work experiences, that fuelled their motivation to keep moving forward when they faced setbacks and roadblocks. On a smaller scale, think about what lengths you've gone to in order not to have to do something? I know I have cleaned the bathroom, done my laundry, cooked food and answered my emails, only to realise that the task I had been putting off wasn't going anywhere.

Procrastination isn't always a bad thing, if you're using that time spent avoiding the "main quest" to pursue useful side quests, that will improve your skills and make the main quest easier. Things like experimenting with plugin chains, watching video tutorials or playing and analysing the soundscape of a new game are all useful things to do with your time, but in order to progress you will have to eventually complete that main quest, no matter how much you try to avoid it.

That's where positive motivation comes in to save the day. I would describe myself as an optimist and a dreamer, overly ambitious and with my head in the clouds most of the time. What I'm pretty good at, though, is knowing exactly *why* I'm doing something and having a clear vision of the bigger picture and how smaller tasks contribute to it. This vision is what drives me – it helps me wake up early in the morning on those icy-cold winter days, when all I want to do is curl up in a ball and go back to sleep.

You may be familiar with the analogy of the carrot and the stick. It has a positive component that you want to chase, and a negative one that you want to avoid. For me, the "carrot" was the prospect of getting my first job in game audio and building a career in which I could progress, grow and be creatively fulfilled. The "stick" was not wanting to have to work a job that drained the joy out of my life and made me miserable. When faced with adversity, having a clear understanding of what motivates us can make it easier to stay focused, or pick ourselves back up when we get knocked down.

Task – The Carrot and the Stick

Take some time to consider what it is that motivates you to begin (or continue on) your game audio journey. Your answers to the previous tasks may help you understand what it is that's driving you if you're unsure. You may find that you have more positive motivations than negative, or vice versa, and that's totally okay – just like our circumstances, our motivations are unique to us.

THE ACTION PLAN

We've covered a lot in a short span of time, so let's recap before we press on. Here are four actionable steps that you can follow to level up your skills and maximise your chances of success along your journey. Don't feel like you have to complete these steps before proceeding, however; we'll be covering a lot of these topics in more detail later on in the book, so the main goal for now is to keep them in mind as you continue.

Learn the Fundamentals

In your game audio journey, the fundamentals are what you rely on most. They are the foundation on which all your other skills are built, and that you will keep going back to. I created *Game Audio Learning* specifically to provide an easy way to learn those fundamentals, so that's where I'd recommend starting out. If you're already in the world of general audio that we discussed earlier, then you may have a good grasp of audio fundamentals already, in which case your goal should be to learn how to apply your knowledge in a new context. The *GAL* website contains all kinds of useful resources and guides as well, so I'd recommend doing as I did and diving right in; immerse yourself in the world of game audio and what it has to offer. Remember, too, that the best way to learn is through a mixture of theory and practice, so read/listen and then apply that knowledge through practical tasks.

Find a Niche

As you spend time learning the fundamentals, you'll start to get an idea of the different specialisations within the industry and can begin to think about what specific niche within game audio appeals to you most. Each specialisation has its own set of required skills that you can focus on developing. For example, sound design positions will require you to create and implement assets using middleware; technical sound design (a different role to just "sound design") is all about scripting and creating systems in game engines; composers need to be able to work to a brief and understand how interactive scores are created and utilised in games. Once again, theory is best paired with practice, so make sure not only to read about these topics but to try them out for yourself, simulating the work that you would do in a professional setting.

Join Communities

Game audio is a highly socially-driven industry, and so networking and participation are vital for anyone looking to build a career in the space. Networking is a skill unto itself – one that we'll be covering later in this book – but for now your focus should be on community. There are plenty of fantastic game audio communities all over the world, across all different social media or even in person, where you can make friends and receive feedback on your work, helping you to improve at a faster pace. I even co-created a social platform specifically for game audio called *Airwiggles*, with spaces for folks who are just starting on their journeys in the industry. When you join one of these communities, it's important to become a part of them rather than just posting your work and asking for feedback. Interact with others, share things that interest and inspire you and generally be sociable. Approach it with the goal of making friends and the rest should come naturally!

Prove Your Skills

Last, but definitely not least, is putting together the materials you need to prove your skills to the world – things like a demo reel, portfolio, CV and potentially a website. Having these ready will allow you to pounce on opportunities whenever they arise. Don't be too precious about your demo reel, especially in the beginning; your skills will improve relatively quickly early on, which will mean regular updates to your reel as you replace old clips with newer, better ones. Building a portfolio without prior job experience might seem challenging, but there are always small indie or community-led projects happening that will welcome new faces, as well as game jams, or even projects you can do entirely independently, such as creating your own sound library, or researching a topic and producing an article or video essay on the topic.

WHAT'S NEXT?

The next chapter is all about learning and developing your skills. We'll discuss some aspects of game audio education that you may not have considered and share some tools to help you get stuff done by working smarter rather than harder.

The Learning Curve

2

EDUCATION

Learning new concepts and skills is an essential part of any journey into a new career, but there are more ways to approach this process than just enrolling on a university course. Don't get me wrong, universities are great; self-directed learning is challenging, and universities can provide some much-needed structure and accountability, as well as the opportunity to measure yourself through exams and against your peers. However, game audio is a relatively new discipline, and so it isn't super well-represented in traditional educational spaces. School and university courses covering audio technology are usually taught from the perspective of music production, with topics important to game audio often missing from the course content.

These courses can still be worthwhile, however, provided you can find ways to make them work for you. Select optional modules that are most relevant to your interests, and request adjustments to assessments where possible to change the focus of your course to align more with your goals. As I mentioned in the previous chapter, this is exactly what I did during my time at university, and the industry-specific experience I was able to gain from doing so was invaluable. Your lecturers are there to help you succeed and will usually be happy to accommodate your goals in any way they can if you're up-front with them about your situation.

If you're looking at university courses and attending open days, take a look at the optional modules available and ask about the possibility of making adjustments to coursework based on your desired career path. It's a lesson that applies to a lot of things in life: you don't ask, you don't get. Being proactive and taking the first step rather than waiting and hoping that something will come to you will benefit you in so many areas of your life.

DOI: 10.1201/9781003368854-3

Self-Directed Learning

While educational courses and programmes dedicated to game audio have become more commonplace in recent years, self-directed learning is still a major part of the process for most if not all folks in game audio. Even if you're enrolled at a university, especially if you're not, you need to be able to dedicate time to studying independently. You don't have to commit hours at a time – just 15 minutes here and there can make a huge difference. You can pick a single topic and deep-dive into it, or take a broader approach and build your general knowledge of audio and game development.

I used to use my findings from searching for junior sound design positions as a jumping-off point for my research. I'd scour the library and internet for any books, videos, interviews and blogs relating to these topics, before opening my DAW and applying what I'd learned. This kind of self-directed learning is an ongoing process, even after you've built yourself a career in the industry. We'll look at it in more depth later on and explore some techniques you can use to get the most out of the process.

Mentorships

A great addition to-or substitute for-structured learning is finding a mentor who has professional experience in your preferred field. They can provide guidance and feedback, impose deadlines to hold you accountable and push you to improve your skills. There are a number of mentorship programmes out there including our own, all of which you can find on the *GAL* website.

Industry Experience

Educational institutions are a valuable source of information and a great way to learn things in a structured environment, but oftentimes the course content alone isn't enough to prepare you for your first job in industry. Knowledge and skills are important, obviously, but first-hand experience is even more valuable when you're pitching yourself to an employer or client.

> I watched so many people go into their 3rd years of university and fail… they didn't consider any of the career stuff.
>
> *Cai Jones*

As we mentioned in our Action Plan at the end of Chapter 1, there are plenty of options for gaining experience independently or in low-pressure team environments. Ideally, you should try to find time to do a few things like this while you're studying. Getting your assignments changed can allow you to produce portfolio-ready material from your coursework, but taking that additional step to produce something in your own time, outside of the confines of a structured educational space, can help to show that you're a self-starter and able to take the initiative, as well as that you're serious about making game audio into a career.

QUANTITY LEADS TO QUALITY

My first attempts at sound design were pretty bad. I was aware they were bad because I knew what "good" sounded like and they didn't sound like that. When I compared my work to the amazing cinematics and trailers made by professionals, it didn't even come close. My expectations were greater than what my skills could achieve, which was frustrating but also, in a way, reassuring. I had an ear for where the quality of my work should be and just needed to continue practising and improving my skills to get there.

David Fairfield describes this as a conflict between "taste and tension." We've all had ideas that sound great in our heads but fail to materialise in the way we'd hoped. The "tension" occurs when our ability to realise our ideas falls short of our ambition – our "taste" (Figure 2.1).

Falling short of the expectations we set for ourselves is disappointing, but we only feel that way because we have taste. We have a vision, the desire to

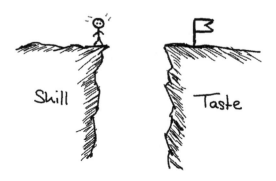

FIGURE 2.1 Tension occurs when our taste exceeds our ability, but the important thing is that you have taste!

create, and we know how our work *should* sound, so all we need to do is "tool up" and improve our skills.

When you start anything new, you'll suck at first, and failures can be especially tough early on, when your taste is so far ahead of your skill. You might have some raw talent which will give you a head-start, but you still won't be as good or experienced as the people who've been doing it for a long time. And that's normal! The key is repetition – trying again and again, learning from your failures each time until eventually, the gap between your taste and your ability shrinks, and one day disappears completely. In short: quantity leads to quality. "Perfect" is the enemy of "finished," so focus on making it better than the last thing you did and get it out the door.

Still to this day, I fail regularly and often when I take on new challenges in my game audio career. The difference is that I'm comfortable doing so, and know that if I trust the process, learn from my mistakes and adjust course, I'll eventually get it right. While writing this chapter, I spent over a week working on the sounds for a feature in a game project my team was working on. After reviewing my work, we ended up sticking with the placeholder sounds we already had, refining and reworking them instead of using my newly made sounds. As you can imagine my ego took a bit of a hit, but my work had still been worthwhile. By exploring and eliminating other options, we had clarified the audio direction for the feature and were able to create a plan to move forward. What felt like a failure to me at that moment was a win for the project as a whole. Later, I continued working on the feature, and with the clear direction that we had established, it was easy to design the rest of the sounds.

Failure can be stressful, but if we reframe it as a learning experience it doesn't have to be. The stakes in game development are incredibly low compared to other fields of work, so don't panic when things go wrong. We're not neurosurgeons or firefighters; the worst that can happen if we get something wrong is making something that sounds bad, or accidentally deleting some work and causing a delay. It might seem counterintuitive to downplay the importance of the work you do, but I find it helpful to have some perspective if things aren't going my way and I get overwhelmed or frustrated.

TOOLS FOR GETTING STUFF DONE

Saying things is easy; actually *doing* things is a lot harder as it requires effort, willpower and discipline. There are, however, ways to reduce the friction and make it easier not only to get started but also to reach the finish line. I've put together a list of some of my favourite tools and methods that help me get stuff done.

FIGURE 2.2   By finding things that inspire you, you give yourself more to work with creatively.

Fill Your Hopper

We all know how much easier it is to create something when we feel inspired, so when inspiration won't come to us, we can go out and seek it. David Fairfield calls this process "filling the hopper," referring to the container on top of a paintball gun that you load the paintballs into. In our case, the "ammunition" is made up of things that inspire us. You can't shoot without ammo, and you can't create without ideas and inspiration (Figure 2.2).

The game audio community has an awesome culture of knowledge sharing that you can use to your advantage, taking inspiration from the cool ideas and nuggets of wisdom other folks share, but your ammunition can come from anywhere – anything that sounds interesting, looks cool or just grabs your attention in some way. The world's full of amazing things, and the more of it you expose yourself to, the more chances you give yourself to find inspiration.

Make Big Monsters Into Little Monsters

When faced with big problems and large tasks it's easy to feel overwhelmed and end up procrastinating as we struggle to figure out where to even start. In these situations, when the goal in front of you is too much to take in at once, we have to break it down into its component steps. To use another of David Fairfield's names, this is the process of "making little monsters out of big monsters," and it's an essential skill in game development.

Start by listing all of the major things that need to happen in order to reach your goal – these are your major milestones. Each of these milestones can then be broken down further into tasks that need to be completed in order for the milestone to be reached. These tasks may have their own subtasks – these are our "little monsters," the smallest elements of our framework and the immediate next steps we can take toward our overarching goal. With our tasks and subtasks laid out, it becomes easier to see what our next step needs to be. Maybe that's recording and sourcing audio to design with, finding references and examples, or even doing some homework on how a gun works to better understand the various mechanical steps involved in creating the sound.

Breaking problems into smaller, actionable steps makes it easy to start moving towards a solution, as you always have a manageable next step you can take, which in turn makes it easier to build momentum and keep moving forward. Writing this book felt like an impossible task when we started, but once Jonny and I broke the journey down into smaller steps, we were able to figure out a path that would get us to the summit, one step at a time. Remember: when staring up at a mountain, the most important step you can take is the one right in front of you.

Task – Little Monsters

Have a go at applying this framework yourself. Take a project or challenge that you're working on and break it down into small, granular steps. What's the overarching goal? What are the milestones that go into achieving that goal? What are the tasks and subtasks necessary to reach those milestones? Don't leave anything out – even the small, easy jobs are worth writing down, as they help you to build momentum to tackle what comes after.

Make It a Game

When faced with too many options, we often experience something called "decision paralysis," finding ourselves unable to choose what to do or where to go because there are simply too many possibilities to choose from. Breaking tasks down into smaller steps can be a big help, as it allows you to focus on what's most important, but it doesn't eliminate all of the different creative paths that we can go down. To help us with that, we can make the process into a game, creating rules that impose creative limitations on us.

This not only makes decisions easier by removing options but also moves us into a state of play, which can enhance one's creativity.[1] We need play in our lives to learn and grow, and that doesn't stop when we're adults.

By introducing rules and restrictions, we can create a game out of an ordinary task, challenging ourselves to get creative and think outside the box. Early on in my sound design career, I started to redesign sounds from games using only a single object as a sound source, for example, creating a sci-fi gun sound using only my house keys. This constraint led me to record, process and manipulate audio in novel ways to get as many interesting sounds as possible from a limited sound source.

To this day, I regularly engage in short play sessions that I call "sound doodles." I set myself a time limit of 15 minutes, choose some additional limitations like only using one type of plugin or a single sound source and then start playing around. In the process, I learn lots of new things, such as how different combinations of plugins sound or what happens when I modulate this or that parameter. This information gets added to my toolbox of techniques and methods which I can use later in my job.

Try some of the following rules and limitations, and see what you can come up with:

- Use only a single sound source.
- Use only white noise as your sound source.
- Use only a single type of plugin (delay, reverb, EQ, etc.).
- Modulate every parameter on a plugin.
- Don't use any plugins.
- Use only musical instruments.

These are all technical constraints, but you can also try more creatively focused challenges, like trying to create a soundscape to accompany a short story or telling a story through sound design without dialogue or music. Of course, I'm writing this from a sound designer's viewpoint, but this technique can be translated into any area of game audio, from technical sound design to music composition or voice acting. If you're not sure which rules to try, write a bunch of them on pieces of paper and choose one at random – the more you can gamify the process, the better.

Be Held Accountable

I used to go to the gym frequently with a friend of mine. We would always go together, even if one of us was tired, because we didn't want to let the other person down. We motivated each other to work harder and push ourselves to our limits, while also just hanging out and having a good time. Then my gym buddy moved away, and I started to really struggle to keep up the good habit. Eventually, I gave it up – without someone there to make sure I went, I wasn't able to motivate myself to do it.

At the time of writing this book, I am working remotely from the comfort of my own home. I love the freedom it brings – the time it saves not having to commute, the ability to tailor my workspace to my needs – but on a bad day, it can feel very isolating and hard to motivate myself, as there is no one around to hold me accountable for the work I need to do. When you work in an office, you're surrounded by colleagues all working together to reach the same goal, which can help motivate you, but if you struggle to motivate yourself and don't have a shared working space, you have to get creative.

Recently, I started doing video calls with a friend of mine who is a music producer. We both sit at home in front of our computers most of the day, so we decided that it would be fun to try doing it together. We don't talk to each other while we're working, but we have our webcams on and when one of us needs a break we stop and have a conversation (we don't share our screens – breaking NDAs isn't part of the exercise!). Having someone there who is also working has made it a lot easier for me to stay focused for longer periods of time and eliminated the feelings of isolation I had been experiencing.

Back in the realm of fitness, I now practise Muay Thai at a local gym, where I have weekly 1-to-1 lessons with a trainer. Having someone who can hold you accountable for your work but also coach you and help you become better at your craft is incredibly valuable. As we mentioned earlier, the world of game audio is similarly full of experienced and friendly folks willing to mentor people who are just starting their journeys in the industry and provide that point of contact to help you motivate yourself.

Make It Easy

When I was in school, I absolutely hated studying for exams – it was an activity I dreaded but couldn't get away from. Rewarding myself after studying wasn't enough to motivate me, so I made the reward part of the activity itself. I got up an extra thirty minutes earlier before school, ran myself a hot bubble bath and studied in the bathtub. This not only aided my focus by helping me to relax, but also made the activity more enjoyable and therefore easier to do.

If you have to write a bunch of cover letters for job applications, instead of doing it at home, go to your favourite coffee shop and write them there with a drink and a snack. If you're learning how a game engine works, instead of sitting in front of your computer alone, invite a friend to join you (online or in person) and learn together. Get creative, have fun, and even the tasks you aren't looking forward to will become a lot easier.

WHAT'S NEXT?

In Chapter 3, we'll be covering the transition into working full-time in the game audio industry – how to find and prepare for opportunities and some of the ways you might look to support yourself as you grow your career.

REFERENCES

1. West, S. (2015) *Playing at Work: Organizational Play as a Facilitator of Creativity*. PhD thesis. Lund University. Available at: https://portal.research. lu.se/en/publications/playing-at-work-organizational-play-as-a-facilitator-of-creativit (Accessed: 09 January 2024).

Hobby to Career

3

During my time in the industry, I've spoken to countless game audio pros about how their careers started out – their experiences, successes and mistakes – and there are some clear patterns and common threads across all of them that I've distilled into five principles that we'll be covering in this chapter. They are as follows:

- Time Liberation
- Generating Income
- Networking
- Preparation
- Perseverance

TIME LIBERATION

Time is a finite resource – there is only so much time available to us on any given day, and so it's up to us to choose how we spend it. The more focused time you invest into doing a task or learning a new skill, the higher the return on that investment. Logically, you will be able to progress a lot faster if you put in 10 hours of practice each week instead of only 2. Your first step, then, is to liberate as much of your time as possible from other tasks and reinvest it into building your career. However, it's absolutely vital to do this in a sustainable way, meaning that:

- You are able to financially support yourself.
- You work at a pace that you can maintain indefinitely, without sacrificing your physical or mental well-being.

The amount of time you are able to invest sustainably will vary from person to person and is something you will have to determine for yourself. If you have relatively few financial responsibilities and a lot of free time, you

 DOI: 10.1201/9781003368854-4

will likely be able to dedicate more time to learning and developing your career than someone who needs to work a "day job" to make rent or support a family. Even if you have all the time in the world, however, it's still important to work at a pace that is sustainable. It may be an old cliché, but the process of building a career in any industry is a marathon, not a sprint, and putting yourself under massive financial strain or overworking yourself for long periods of time will eventually cause you to burn out. If that happens, you won't be in a position to pursue a job, much less build a career.

When a good friend of mine started pursuing his game audio career he went all-in. He quit his job and fully committed himself to somehow "making it work." The pressure was incredibly high, which drove him to work tirelessly and say yes to every opportunity that came along, even if it was a bad one. Eventually, the stress became overwhelming, to the point that he thought about quitting the industry for good. Thankfully, he was able to find an in-house position which was a great fit for him, but even after leaving freelancing behind it was hard for him to slow down and avoid overworking himself at his new job – old habits die hard. Looking back, he asked himself "What have I sacrificed for this?" He told me that if he did it all again, he would do it slower, keep his part-time job for longer, and not sprint away from the starting line.

A lot of my other friends started with a slower pace which they could maintain. They didn't go all-in immediately and had regular incomes from stable second jobs that kept them above water in tougher times. As they grew their network and gained more opportunities, they reduced their hours at their day jobs to liberate more time for game audio, and eventually transitioned into doing game audio full-time. Finding a sustainable level of activity and thinking long-term is vital to both your career success and your well-being.

GENERATING INCOME

In order to do game audio full-time, you need to earn enough money to sustain yourself. You can build up your income from game audio gradually, using the time you liberate to improve your skills while doing another job on the side to support yourself.

Part-Time Jobs

I used to work at my university's coffee shop, as well as a fast-food restaurant, to keep my finances stable. Once I got some audio projects in, I cut down my hours and eventually dropped the fast-food gig completely.

My university also asked me to do some hours as a custodian, handing out music equipment, locking and unlocking the studios and cleaning the classrooms at the end of the day. This worked brilliantly for me because there would be large periods of time where very little happened, allowing me to work on game audio and university assignments while still getting paid. One of my friends worked in the university library and was similarly able to work on assignments and music in their DAW during quiet periods.

There are a number of jobs that mainly require you to be there but not to actually do a lot of hard work. During the downtime, you can work on your own projects, or if you don't have access to a computer, you can read books and articles, or sketch out audio systems on paper. I'm not telling you to slack off at your job – on the contrary, the more efficient you are, the more time you'll have to do your own thing!

Audio and Gamedev-Related Jobs

There are a multitude of jobs in the fields of audio and game development which you can do while transitioning into a full-time career. These jobs may not necessarily be what you want to be doing in the long term, but they can be preferable to other traditional part-time jobs in the retail or service industries and can provide some valuable game industry experience to put on your CV.

Roles like QA Tester and Localisation Tester can be great ways to get your foot in the door and start meeting people in the games industry, but don't underestimate the value of jobs in adjacent industries – editing dialogue for film/TV or podcasts can provide valuable experience and even some credits if you're lucky. Additionally, if you have a music background or play an instrument, tuition can be a great source of income, giving either 1-to-1 or group lessons. If, like me, you're not good with instruments, then teaching basic audio skills and how to use DAWs can also work, though the target audience isn't as large.

Freelancing

Whether your long-term goal is to find an in-house position or be a full-time freelancer, taking on projects and contract work is an excellent way to gain experience, grow your portfolio and earn money in the process. By having worked on actual projects and potentially gained credits on a shipped title or two, you'll have an edge when applying to junior positions.

If you want to be a freelancer in the first place, then the sooner you start, the better – every job is an opportunity to build your client base, learn how to manage projects and improve your skills. If you can, try teaming up with other freelancers with different skill sets – sound designers, audio programmers, composers and so on – as an informal collective of professionals. You don't have to be a corporate entity, but you can share networks, recommend each other for jobs and work with bigger clients as a team. You can find more advice specific to freelancing in the game audio industry on the *GAL* website.

Creating Your Own Business

Going freelance full-time requires a lot of different skills in addition to simply being able to do the job, as you're basically running your own business. There are business opportunities in the industry beyond just freelancing as a sound designer or composer, however, such as creating sound libraries, developing plugins and other software, running a recording studio or equipment rental services. The competition can be fierce, so I wouldn't personally suggest this approach as a way to enter the industry, but I think it's important to acknowledge that it can work, with the right combination of unique ideas and a little luck. If you're an enterprising type and you see a gap in the market, then why not have a go?

NETWORKING

Networking is, if you boil it down, all about the people we meet and the things we share with them. A strong network is one full of friends and people that you've built meaningful relationships with, all of whom are rooting for you and want you to succeed. The key word here is *friends* – a friend will recommend you for an opportunity because they trust you and want to help you. A random person who you've handed a business card to doesn't have any reason or incentive to do the same, which is why it's absolutely crucial to approach networking as an exercise in making friends, developing relationships and ultimately building trust. It can sound daunting on paper, but it's as simple as showing up to regular events and getting to know people, instead of just rocking up and asking for a job. These events might be for game audio folks, but there's nothing stopping you from talking about your other hobbies and interests and asking the people you meet about theirs (Figure 3.1).

Once you've made friends in these spaces, opportunities will start to appear as people recommend you for jobs they hear about. I got my first paid contract this way, through a friend of mine called Lewis Thompson, whom

FIGURE 3.1   *Networking* doesn't necessarily mean talking about work.

I met at a local networking event he had organised and I found online. We immediately formed a bond, and he brought me along to other events where I met his friends, who eventually invited me to a regular board game night. They were all either already in the games industry or on the brink of getting in. One day, Lewis received an offer for a freelance project but was too busy to take it on. We had become close friends over the course of a year, and so he trusted me enough to recommend me instead. This ended up becoming my first big paid game development project, which was a stepping stone to further, bigger projects.

Be Part of the Community

In addition to the people we meet, what we choose to share with the world is an important part of how we network. During 2020, I started gradually building my online presence, including making YouTube videos about game audio, which ended up being the deciding factor in landing my first full-time position at a small start-up game developer. Each thing that we share contributes to the impression of us that the world sees – redesigns, technical demonstrations, articles and even simple things such as commenting and giving feedback on someone else's work. You don't have to start a YouTube channel or any other huge endeavour to start building your presence. All it takes is to show up – both online and offline – and interact with the community you want to be a part of. Add value to the community by being friendly and helping others. Put yourself and your work out there to actively seek feedback and improve.

Our network is not just there to catch opportunities but also to support us in harder times, help us grow and fulfil our human needs of friendship and connection. Having a peer group is a great way to develop, allowing you to measure yourselves and learn from each other. This is especially important if you are a freelancer who often works solo and is reliant on a constant flow of work rather than a yearly salary. You can find a guide to networking using social media and a list of common pitfalls to avoid on the *GAL* website.

Start Now

It is *never* too early to start networking. Even if you're still studying, even if you haven't worked on a completed project yet, the sooner you can start meeting people and making connections, the better. There are plenty of folks out there at a similar point in their journeys to you, and getting to know others in your position can lead to all kinds of opportunities, both to learn and grow and also to find work. If nothing else, the game audio community is a friendly and welcoming one, so there's no reason not to get involved!

Don't say you're an 'aspiring' sound designer, just say you're a sound designer… don't gatekeep yourself.

Lewis Thompson

Be Proactive

Making connections and being community-minded are both important steps, but they won't guarantee you opportunities. Some might come to you without much input, but to get the most out of networking you have to be *proactive*. My first full-time job that I mentioned earlier came from me taking the initiative and chasing what I thought was a potential opportunity. I had struck up a conversation with a developer at a leaving party for a friend of mine and after having a great conversation in person, I emailed him the next day, having found out he had worked on one of my favourite games of my childhood. He asked me what I thought of the audio, and I sent him two pages of feedback notes plus a link to my YouTube channel. In retrospect, it was probably a little over the top, but it worked in my favour, and a couple of weeks later he offered me an interview and then a job working with him on his next project.

Make the most of what's in front of you right now.

Sergio Ronchetti

The key takeaway from this story is that you have to follow up with people. If you meet someone at an event, message them on social media later – initiate contact and show them that you're interested in staying in touch. If they mention a project and you're interested in the work, tell them! Consider how you can add value to someone's work or a project and approach them with an idea – there's no shame in asking for work, so long as you're respectful in doing so. Of course, it is important to be considerate, both in how you communicate but also in the potential opportunities you try to follow. For example, it is considered inappropriate by some to "cold call" prospective clients, who haven't discussed their project with you already and aren't publicly hiring people, or to approach a developer that you know already has someone contracted to do the work – attempting to undercut people will make you very unpopular.

How To Get Lucky

Throughout the interviews I conducted for this book, every person's story had some version of "I was in the right place at the right time," or "I got lucky and it all lined up perfectly." Indeed, those are the sentences I use when telling the story of how my own career in game audio got started. Relying on luck to hand us a career doesn't sound like a brilliant strategy, so instead, let's create our own. As the old adage says, "Luck is what happens when preparation meets opportunity."

The Right Place

Video games are a globe-spanning industry, but you will often find areas where the industry's presence is denser, and opportunities are more abundant. These are "industry hubs," formed over time as successful companies attract talent to an area, which in turn draws more companies to that area, creating a positive feedback loop of growth. These hubs can be found all over the world, with countries like the USA, France, Germany, the UK and Japan having especially large ones. If your country has any notable gaming industry hubs, then moving closer to one can be a path toward more opportunities.

If moving isn't an option, however, then fear not – it is still possible to network effectively away from an industry hub, attending gamedev events and conferences that are closer to home, or even online. More and more, people are making their start in the world of game audio entirely through online networking, the advent of social media and working from home making it easier than ever to meet people and find work through "virtual industry hubs" on platforms like LinkedIn or Airwiggles – a site created by me and Lewis Thompson specifically for the game audio community. You can find groups on most social platforms with a quick search for "gamedev" or "game audio." I'd recommend joining only 1 or 2 groups to begin with and making an effort to be active and get to know people in those groups – joining too many groups at once may make it difficult to engage meaningfully with any of them. Additionally, be sure to check out the Airwiggles event calendar for upcoming events around the world.

The Right Time

As we build our network and establish our presence in the community, soon enough, opportunities will begin to present themselves, and it's important that we are prepared to grab them when they do. However, it's vital not to confuse "being prepared" with "feeling ready." You might never feel fully ready for an opportunity – I certainly didn't when I got my first full-time job in game audio – but in order to grow we sometimes need to push the boundaries we've set for ourselves, which can mean doing things we don't always feel ready for. If we don't take that step beyond what we're totally comfortable with, it may never feel like "the right time" and opportunities may pass us by. There is an antidote to that feeling of unreadiness, however: preparation.

PREPARATION

In the face of doubt and anxiety, making sure that we are prepared gives us the best possible chance of succeeding. It's a great way to combat feelings of uncertainty and stress because you can reassure yourself that you have the knowledge and skills you need to achieve what you set out to do. You can even practise exact steps for some situations, making the real thing just a matter of going through the motions.

Imagine you have an interview for your dream job. It would be totally understandable to be nervous – you might try not to think about it and avoid worrying yourself, but then you would risk going into the interview unprepared and being blindsided by questions you aren't expecting. Imagine instead that you take the time to do some homework, learn more about the company's history and current projects, practise answering some common interview questions, and so on. Chances are you'll still be nervous, but you can take some comfort from knowing that you are prepared and able to improvise if any tricky questions are thrown at you.

How to Prepare

If someone challenged you to race, you'd need to know what kind of race they had in mind in order to prepare yourself – a motor race? A marathon? An all-stars speedrun of *Super Mario 64*? Similarly, not all opportunities are alike, and so the steps you'll need to take to prepare will depend on the types of opportunity you decide to pursue. Start by asking yourself what sort of opportunity it is you want to chase – AAA or indie, freelance or in-house – and consider what kinds of situations and challenges you would expect to face in doing so.

This is where research comes into play – information is your biggest ally, and knowing what to expect is often half the battle. Consider the audio test, for example – these are a relatively common part of the job application process in game audio, but if you've not done one before, or don't know what's involved, you might be caught off-guard and lose position to someone who's done some practice audio tests in their own time. With a bit of research, you can learn what audio tests are all about, what to expect, and what employers are looking for.

The more questions you can ask yourself, and the more homework you can do to find the answers, the better. What sort of questions might a AAA developer ask you in an interview? What kind of deadline would an indie developer expect you to work to, and how much should you charge? With this information in mind, you can put together a game plan and go into an interview prepared, which will give you confidence. Bonus points if you do a couple of mock interviews with friends or family to practise answering the questions aloud. If you're a freelancer, it's especially worth thinking about money – what rates you will charge, whether to ask for a deposit and how much, and so on. Create a project proposal template and draft up a contract you can present to clients; there are plenty of great templates online to modify as you need.

The more prepared you feel, the easier it will be to stay relaxed during the interview and present the best version of yourself to an employer – after all, doing anything for the first time is going to be harder than if you've practised beforehand. As well as learning the processes involved, one especially useful thing you can do to prepare yourself for opportunities is to create a profile on a platform such as LinkedIn or Soundlister, with all of your information and your demo reel easily accessible. You could even create your own website to act as a sort of "digital business card," with your reel, portfolio and CV all in one place. As mentioned earlier, you can find information and advice for interview preparation, as well as the business side of freelancing, on the *GAL* website.

PERSEVERANCE

It may sound incredibly obvious, but persisting in the face of setbacks is the most important – and the hardest – part of getting into the industry. It takes resilience to chase a career in the games industry, and sadly there's no quick hack or secret to it. All you can do is manage your expectations, believe in yourself and focus on the steps we've discussed in this chapter. It's important to remember that everyone's path is unique to them – I've asked countless game audio professionals how long it took them to make the transition into working full-time in the industry. On average, it took most people 3–6 years to build a sustainable career. Most of these people were working part-time jobs and slowly increasing their game audio work year by year, until they landed a full-time position or had enough projects to sustain themselves as freelancers. It can be a slow process, but slow progress is still progress, and you'll never arrive at your destination if you stop walking.

As a society we have a bad habit of romanticising the "leap of faith" – quitting your job to pursue your dreams and just hoping for the best. It might sound exciting, but it's rarely healthy or sustainable – it's quicker to skydive without a parachute, but the goal isn't just to reach the ground quickly, it's to reach it safely and relish the view. Focus on your trajectory, not your current position. Go at your own pace and enjoy the ride, because ultimately everything in life will be an experience to look back at, and the destination isn't worth spoiling the journey for yourself.

WHAT'S NEXT?

Our next chapter is all about finding your feet as you start working in the industry. We'll be going over what to do (and what not to do) as you get yourself up to speed in your first few months.

You've Got the Job! Now What?

4

Congratulations, you've got your first game audio job! Strap in and hold on tight, because the real learning and fun starts now! Here's how not to fall on your face in your first month on the job.

AM I THE IMPOSTOR?

Doing anything for the time can be nerve-wracking, but when it's the thing you're most passionate about, the pressure is even more intense. You want to prove to your team – and to yourself – that you truly belong there, and that motivation is a good thing, but that internal pressure can easily turn into anxiety if not managed, making the experience unpleasant and preventing you from doing your best work. Trust me, I know because I've been there. I've felt like a fraud, like my work wasn't good enough and that I didn't belong, that it was only a matter of time before I was "found out" and fired. I had self-doubt, and lots of it!

It turns out that I wasn't alone in feeling this way, and neither are you – everyone I've spoken to in this industry, from juniors to industry veterans, has experienced it at some point in their careers. A lot of them still do on a regular basis – myself included – when starting a new project, a new job, or simply doing a task that I've never done before. This feeling has a name which you might have heard before: Impostor syndrome. Although the feeling might be bad, we can take away a silver lining from it – in order to grow we have to push ourselves out of our comfort zones, and that uncomfortable feeling is a sign that you're doing exactly that. While the feeling may never truly go away, we can reassure ourselves knowing that the struggle is in service of self-improvement.

DOI: 10.1201/9781003368854-5

A CHANCE MEETING

My first full-time job in the games industry wasn't actually working in game audio. It started when I met industry veteran Sean Cooper at a friend's leaving party. We got along well, and I learned that he was in the process of creating a new startup company for a game project. He had assembled a small team with a tonne of experience but was missing someone who could take care of the audio. After a lot of back-and-forth emails (including my aforementioned two pages of audio feedback), we built up a good relationship, and when the time came, I had a formal interview with him, which was successful. I did two weeks of freelance work, creating audio for the initial prototype of the game. There were some hurdles, but with the help of more experienced friends whom I reached out to, I managed to overcome them. So far, so good. Sean told me to keep in touch as there might be more work on the horizon, and so I did.

A couple of months later, I got a message from Sean asking if I knew any good junior game designers that I could introduce him to, so I started reaching out to friends. One of them was interested, but when the time came and we all got together at a games event, my friend informed me that he had just accepted a full-time offer from another company. I broke the news to Sean and didn't think too much of it. Later that evening we were talking about the position again and he asked me, "Are *you* any good at game design?"

"Well, I've never done it before, but I'll give it a shot." I replied.

He nodded. "Alright, let's give it a shot, I reckon I can train you up. When can you start?"

And with those words I had accepted my first full-time game development job… as a game designer?

In at the Deep End

At this point I didn't just *feel* like an impostor – when it came to game design, I literally was one, with no prior knowledge or experience, but I trusted Sean's judgement to hire me, and that with his mentorship and guidance I would be able to make a positive contribution to the project. The small team of four I was working with had over 100 years of industry experience between them, but none of them were avid gamers anymore. I was, and that was what made me valuable to the team. We spent a couple of months building and refining our demo and started pitching it to publishers, including some big AAA ones. Pitching a game is kind of like going on Shark Tank or one of those similar

TV shows, where a person comes in with a business idea and has to convince investors to give them their money. Like in the show, they shoot holes in the idea, ask difficult questions, and gauge how prepared you are to solve the potential problems that may arise. As the team's dedicated game designer, I was responsible for answering a lot of these questions, especially when it came to the current market and our competitors.

Every pitch meeting was incredibly scary, and I remember vividly how out of place I felt during our first pitch, as we introduced ourselves alongside a presentation slide with all of our names and qualifications. Mine said "Audio design background, experience working in indie development, avid gamer (in touch with current trends) and well-connected in the Guildford games community," while the ones next to me said things like "30+ years in the industry, multi-award-winning including BAFTA, etc." But to my surprise, the people across the table took me seriously, and my team trusted me to deliver. At first it was tough, but the more we did it the better the pitch got, and with experience came confidence, and the feeling of impostor syndrome diminished. I became comfortable tackling the ever-present new challenges that the job threw at me, and started to recognise the value that I brought to the team. Our pitch became well-rehearsed, and I was no longer just "the new guy" – by this time I had more experience pitching than a lot of game developers would have during their entire career.

THE LESSONS LEARNED

As you can probably tell, that year working with Sean was a real voyage into the unknown for me. While I was out of my depth at first, the experience taught me a lot about what it's like to begin a career in this industry. Here are some of the biggest things I learned during that year...

Take the Plunge

I still regularly get a wave of anxiety before doing something for the first time, sharing my work online, or sometimes when it's time for my work to be reviewed by my lead. Unfortunately, it's an unavoidable part of working in a creative industry like game development. We are usually our own harshest critics, and it's easy to compare ourselves to others and be left feeling deflated, especially in the age of social media, where other people's incredible work seems to be all around us. For me, one of the best ways to combat impostor syndrome has been to, as the slogan says, *just do it*. Take the leap and get started with that new task, hit send on that social media post, go into that review, and do it again and again and again. Over time, you get used to the feeling, and it loses its power over you. It's become one of my trusty travel companions – when it's there I know that I'm on the right path, a guiding star leading me out of my comfort zone towards growth and improvement.

Be Patient with Yourself

No matter how much you study, practise and prepare for a career in game audio, your first job will always be a learning experience. You can read a game's controls in the manual (ask your parents), but you'll still need time to build muscle memory and learn how to apply combos and strategies effectively – give yourself time to learn!

> When I first took dancing lessons with my wife, I was awful at it. Then again, when is anyone good at something that they've never done before? We're okay with this dynamic in regular life, why shouldn't we cut ourselves a break when it comes to a new part of our career journey?
>
> *David Fairfield*

Look How You've Grown

Another great exercise to do from time to time is comparing your current work to your past work. Listen to your old projects, analyse them, think about what you'd do differently or better today and appreciate how far you've come. Improvement in a skill is such a gradual process that it can be hard to notice until you look back and see the difference between things months or years apart. Take the time to reflect on how you've improved, and allow yourself to feel proud of what you've achieved.

Sharing Is Caring

A strategy to combat impostor syndrome which I use regularly is talking to friends and sharing your struggles. You might feel like you're burdening your friends by telling them these things, but it's often the exact opposite. Opening up and being vulnerable gives them a chance to do the same and share their experiences with you, leaving you both feeling better. Especially when talking with friends who are also in the industry, it can be cathartic to share with people who know how it feels and can relate to what you're telling them.

(Don't) Tell Me Lies

After being hired for my first job, I felt a huge pressure to know everything – when asked "Can you do this?" my first instinct was to say yes and then try to blag my way through it somehow. It wasn't because I was incompetent or a liar, but rather terrified that if I admitted to not knowing something I'd be "found out" as a fraud and fired. This came to a head in my first week as a game designer, when Sean asked me to do something I had no idea how to do. I must have hesitated for a little too long before giving him a timid yes, because he clearly didn't buy it. He asked me again, followed by "It's no problem if you don't know." I confessed that I didn't know, and what he said next has stuck with me ever since:

> Never lie to me, you're just wasting both our time. If you don't know how to do something that's not an issue, I'll either explain it to you or give you time to figure it out and learn.

Now that I'm not a junior anymore and have worked with people less experienced than myself, I realise that I was foolish to think like that in the first place. I was hired for a reason and Sean was very aware of my skills, or lack thereof. In my more experienced position today, I would never expect anyone who has just been hired to know everything. Quite the opposite, in fact – I would want them to ask as many questions as possible, be keen to learn, and be clear about what they don't know so I could help them learn. The whole idea of hiring someone junior is to train them up to become an experienced member of the team. There would be no point in hiring a junior who knows everything already – they wouldn't be a junior. Remember: you've been hired for who *you* are and what *you* can do. You're not expected to know or be able to do everything immediately – just be patient with yourself and honest with others.

Questions > Assumptions

When we are given a task – to create some sound effects or music for a new feature, for example – it can be tempting to simply go away for a week, get stuck in and come back with some awesome, polished work that you can show off to your team. However, by doing that we run the risk of going in a different creative direction to what was expected of us and having to scrap all of our hard work. This is why it's important to check in regularly and ask questions instead of making assumptions – by sharing a work in progress with your co-workers/client/boss, you give them a chance to offer feedback, and for

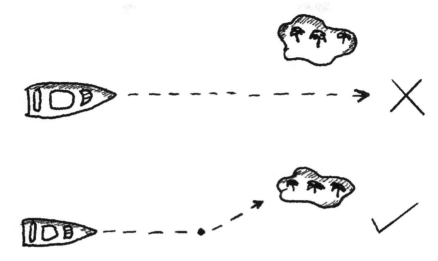

FIGURE 4.1 *The further* you go without checking in, the further from the mark you risk being.

you to change your approach if what you've made so far doesn't meet their expectations. Imagine that you were captaining a ship, and set your heading slightly incorrectly. The further you travel before checking that you're headed the right way, the further off-course you will end up (Figure 4.1).

The bigger the task is, and the further you go without checking, the greater the damage that can be caused by a difference in understanding. Questions don't have to be about the creative direction of a task specifically; sometimes it's worth asking just to avoid wasting your time: Is this task a high priority, or can it wait? Are the animations finalised, or are they still subject to change and will need re-syncing later? Do we need to build a new system for this feature, or is there an existing one that can do the job for us? Questions save time and avoid stress or conflict down the line, so ask away! Remember: it's better to ask a stupid question than make a stupid mistake.

WHAT'S NEXT?

In Chapter 5, we'll be talking about the importance of being a team player, both to your career as a whole but also to the well-being of you and your team, and the quality of the work you do together.

How to be a Team Player

5

Unless you're a solo developer, you'll be working with a team of people in your role as an audio professional. These might be small or large, from one other person to hundreds across all kinds of other disciplines. The best games are made by the best teams, so learning how to be a good teammate is not only essential to your job but also to your long-term career.

YOUR REPUTATION PRECEDES YOU

- Why do some people get better opportunities than others with the same skill level?
- Why do some people get hired without having to do an audio test?
- Why do some people have a loyal client base that returns to them?
- Why do some people only get one-off jobs while others build sustainable careers?
- Why do some people command more authority and respect than others?

The reason some folks move forward where others seemingly don't is the "trust factor." Whether you're a freelancer working with clients and outsourcers or part of a big team at a AAA studio, your reputation precedes you. Despite the fast pace at which the industry moves and grows, the audio community is very close-knit and word spreads quickly, so building a good reputation is one of the most important things you can do for your career. A good reputation is built by earning people's trust, which is the foundation of any relationship, including those with your employer, clients and co-workers.

People who trust you will:

- Offer you work they think you are capable of, leading to more opportunities for you.

DOI: 10.1201/9781003368854-6

- Let you take ownership of tasks and make decisions, granting you more authority and control.
- Ask you for your opinions and advice, making you a more valuable member of the team.
- Want to work with you again in the future, ensuring yet more opportunities down the road.

So how do you earn people's trust? The answer is over long periods of time, through:

- Communication – are you forthcoming with and receptive to information and feedback? Are you honest with people and able to be truthful in a way that's considerate of others?
- Reliability and consistency – can people count on you to show up on time and ready to work? Do your words align with your actions?
- Attitude – are you proactive, willing to pitch in and approach a task head-on, no matter what it is?
- Morale – are you a positive influence? Do you contribute to a positive culture and atmosphere within your team?

In the coming chapter, we're going to tackle each of these areas so that you can build trust and be a great teammate!

COMMUNICATION

Getting a game development deal signed is always a very long-winded process. After nearly a year of working with Sean, we were making great progress with a publisher and getting incredibly close to securing a contract. What we couldn't have foreseen was the COVID-19 pandemic and the disruption it would bring to the world at large and the games industry specifically. This eventually also affected us, as we ran out of money before we signed a publishing deal. Since we didn't know how long the pandemic would last, we had to put the project on hold indefinitely, and I had to go job hunting again. I applied to every position I could find and was either rejected or completely ignored each time. Things were looking bleak, but just as time was running out and the door to my previous job was about to close, another one opened. My good friend Lewis told me about a junior opening at his employer Soundcuts, an audio outsourcing company specialising in games. I applied for it and secured an interview.

An interview is the first time your would-be future employer and co-workers get a chance to see what you're about, test your communication skills and consider how you would fit into the team. They are a skill like any other, which you can practise and improve through mock interviews or just experience through repetition. After a year of pitching to publishers, I was well-practised in talking the talk; now it was just a matter of preparation. I wrote down a bunch of potential questions that I might be asked and went over them again and again. The preparation paid off, and I got the job. Where before I was part of a five-man development team, I now found myself in a team of ten audio specialists working with both small and large studios. Thankfully, they had an experienced leadership team, but also some other juniors with whom I could grow together. It was the perfect environment to develop my skills, and communication was one of them.

Vocabulary

Like most specialised fields, there is a language of game development, and within it "dialects" for each discipline with even more specific words. These words often contain a lot of technical information and context within them, making them extremely useful – even necessary – when communicating with others in game audio, so familiarising yourself with this vocabulary is an essential step in developing your communication skills. Happily, you can improve your game audio vocabulary as you would in any other language – by watching talks, reading articles, asking questions and listening carefully to the answers. Beyond the realm of audio, learning about other disciplines will help you understand their workflows and how they impact yours, so stay curious!

Keep It Simple, Stupid!

While often essential, technical jargon can sometimes hinder more than it helps, when we *think* we understand a term, but are in fact using it incorrectly. This kind of miscommunication occurs most commonly when talking to people from other disciplines, especially programmers. I've fallen into this trap many times, wanting to look smart and explain what I needed from them in technical terms, only to confuse us both when I used the vocabulary wrong. When these misunderstandings happened, I assumed that I just needed to learn *even more* technical terminology in order to explain what I wanted clearly. In reality, I was totally wrong, and the opposite was true. I talked to a good friend of mine who is a senior gameplay programmer, and he told me:

Say the problem, not the solution.

I usually went to a programmer when I had a problem, but instead of telling them what the problem was, I told them what (I thought) the solution was, and what they needed to do to fix it. In retrospect, it's obvious that this was a terrible strategy – programmers are hired for a reason, and you're not there to do their job. When I started to give them the simplest explanation of my issue and what I was trying to achieve, I was surprised how much more success I had. The number of miscommunications dropped drastically, and the programmers usually had a better and more efficient solution than what I would have suggested anyway.

By letting them do their job and focusing on mine, the results were better, and the relationship between us improved as well. We've all seen comments on social media from people who think they know better than professionals. No one wants to deal with armchair programmers, so keep it simple. State the problem as simply as you can, and give the specialists the creative freedom to problem-solve (Figure 5.1).

FIGURE 5.1 Learning the various technical terms unique to game development – and when to keep things simple – is essential in order to communicate effectively with others.

More Than Words

Sometimes, words alone aren't enough to convey an idea. In these cases, we can use visuals and audio in addition to support what we say. When I write documentation, I always try to include diagrams and illustrations that help the reader understand what I'm trying to say. This is something I learned while I was pitching – explaining a concept is good, but planting an image in someone's head and then building on it with words is even better. When it comes to talking about sounds, using words as descriptors can be especially tricky, so I often use my mouth to make sounds that help me convey my ideas. You don't have to be a champion beatboxer or anything – some basic sounds to give an idea of cadence or "vibe" can go a long way in illustrating an idea.

Relationships

By talking to our co-workers, clients and peers regularly, we are able to build strong relationships with them. Everyone prefers working with people that they know and like, and it's a lot easier to ask a friend for a favour than a stranger. Making friends across the development team – outside of audio – can be incredibly useful, especially with people in high-impact disciplines like VFX or animation, which are usually directly before audio in the development pipeline. This allows us to collaborate and work more closely with them, and hopefully be informed about any changes before they happen. Additionally, if we help people from other disciplines understand the role of audio, and how their work impacts ours, we give them a better chance of helping us. People generally enjoy being helpful, especially if they like you.

On top of that, work is just more enjoyable when you get on with your co-workers. Being able to crack jokes and banter with your colleagues is not only fun, but it also helps stop people from taking themselves or each other too seriously, and it's good to combat an egocentric workplace. A bunch of strong egos is the last thing you need in any team environment, as we need to work together and support each other. At the end of the day, everything we do is in service of making the game better, and sometimes people need a playful reminder of that. Don't be afraid to reach out to your co-workers and start a conversation; you'll most likely have a lot in common with the people around you – we're all video game nerds, after all.

It's important to remember, however, that people are different and communicate in different ways. I have friends who use emoji a lot in their messages, which makes them very expressive, and others who like to put a period after every sentence, which can make them sound very blunt and

FIGURE 5.2 Misunderstandings can sometimes happen due to differences in how people communicate.

straightforward. Your tone of voice when you speak and the way you text can have a big impact on how others interpret what you say, so be mindful of the tone you use, both in person and through text (Figure 5.2).

Listening

Listening plays a crucial role in communication, obviously. Nowadays, however, it often comes in the form of reading messages. With remote or hybrid work becoming more popular, face-to-face conversations are less common than they were, happening instead through text channels like Slack, Teams or Discord. This has its upsides, of course – being able to read messages from outside of the audio-specific channels can be incredibly useful, as vital information often doesn't make it to the audio team until the work is right in front of us. It's a common cliché among audio folks that we're always the last to hear anything, and there is unfortunately a lot of truth in that. We have to keep our ears to the ground and actively seek out information, so it pays to help ourselves and have eyes and ears in as many chats and groups as we can. Reading what the artists, animators, programmers and VFX designers are up to can help us plan and manage our upcoming tasks and prevent work from falling through the cracks.

When it comes to listening, there can often be misunderstandings. That's normal, they happen, but there's an easy and simple trick to avoid them: clarify. Sum up what you just heard and repeat it back to the person talking to you – "So basically, you're saying that…" By summarising the information, you're not only more likely to retain it, but you give your colleague the opportunity to add details or clear up any misunderstandings – "Yes, and…" or "No, but…"

RELIABILITY AND CONSISTENCY

If you get on a bus at its first stop in the morning, chances are it will be on time, but if you get on at a later stop along the route, the chances of having to wait increase. There might be traffic or a busy stop with lots of people getting on and off, so the bus gets delayed by one minute here, 2 minutes there. By the time the last stop comes along, those short delays have accumulated and you stand there waiting for a long time. In game development, audio is the very last discipline in the production pipeline – we have to wait for everyone else to be finished with their work before we can finalise ours. Every delay throughout the process accumulates and eventually impacts us, so it's crucial that we don't create any more delays for ourselves. Having teammates that you can rely on to show up and be there to put out fires day after day is necessary.

Imagine if a bus company could send out a second bus to help the first if it got delayed – this would stop the snowballing effect of the delays before they became unmanageable. The same principle applies to working in an audio team – if one person falls behind, other team members can step in to help. If you're alone on a team, you might still be able to give and receive help from other disciplines, probably not by coding or 3D modelling, but maybe by putting together a draft email, writing documentation, or similar tasks that relieve some of the workload for others. By making yourself useful wherever you can, and being the one helping others, you'll be the one people will want on their team, and more opportunities will come to you.

Being reliable also means that your words align with your actions – you say what you're going to do and then you do it. This doesn't mean that you can't make mistakes, but it means that you can be trusted to commit to a task and give everything your best shot – people who aren't reliable don't last long in this industry. Managing your time properly is another essential skill – people are busy, and making your teammates wait for you to join a meeting or taking forever to reply to messages is disrespectful to them. If, like me, you're not good at remembering things, create a system where you don't have to rely on your brain. For me, that's using a calendar app to record meetings and set reminders for things I have to do, but it can be a notepad, voice recorder –whatever helps you stay organised.

ATTITUDE

"Hey Greg, I know you've never done this before but could you do X for me?"

- "Do I have to?"
- "I guess so…"
- "Sure thing, I'll give it my best shot!"

Which Greg would you want to work with? Personally, I'd choose the third option, as he seems enthusiastic and up for the task.

Attitude, mindset, outlook, demeanour – these are all words for the way you approach situations, and how you react to the things happening to you and around you. Attitude isn't binary, however – although we often think in terms of good or bad, positive or negative, it's rarely that simple. It's a sliding scale that can be influenced in the short and long term, by internal and external factors – everything from feeling hungry or tired, to hearing bad news, to misplacing our keys.

Sometimes we just have bad days, and that's fine. What I want to talk about is how you view your work and the people around you on a broader level. Are you making it easy for other people to work with you, or are you actively making it harder?

- Are you up for a challenge, or do you avoid pushing yourself?
- Do you actively seek out work when you've nothing to do, or wait around until prompted to do something by someone else?
- Do you seek out and implement feedback, or try to avoid it?
- Are you able to voice frustrations in a constructive manner and offer solutions, or are you just complaining without making an effort to improve the situation?

People who have a good attitude and are easier to work with and better teammates than those who don't – they are constructive and move forward by themselves. People who are hard to work with drain our energy – they are unmotivated and have to be pushed and prompted to do things. This doesn't mean you have to be bursting with enthusiasm at all times, and always excited to take on the next task. You're allowed to be frustrated when things go wrong and have a rant every once in a while – it's good to get these feelings out so you don't have to sit on them – but when working with others you have to consider your teammates. We can't always control the situation, but we can control how we react to it and the decisions we make.

I've seen people not get hired and even get fired for having a bad attitude towards work and their co-workers. No one wants to work with someone who sends a strong message that they don't want to be there – this is an industry full of passionate people who, for the most part, love their job. The good news is that you're very likely to be one of those passionate people and already have a great attitude. If not then don't worry, because it's something that can be worked on and improved! Even if we can't change a situation, we can always change our mindset and the way we approach it. Mental exercises like mindfulness and practising gratitude can go a long way in helping to challenge negative attitudes and find healthier outlooks.

Try reframing your work as a team sport where the goal is to create a great game. Your decisions and actions should be informed by questions like "how can we as a team make this the best game possible?" and "is this making the game and the team better?" If you're in a situation that you're unsure how to navigate, ask yourself these questions and let the answers help guide you – your best chances of succeeding come when you work with rather than against one another. The same attitude works when applying for jobs, the question being "how can I be the kind of person that others want on their team?"

MORALE

Morale is the overall mood and confidence of a team. It's made up of the attitudes of individuals, how they feel about their situation and how they react to it. Your attitude can have a positive or negative impact on morale, raising or lowering the mood of the people who work with you. A team with high morale can more easily navigate difficult situations by working together, creating a better environment for everyone involved and leading to higher-quality work. Conversely, a team with low morale is more likely to crumble under pressure when faced with challenging situations.

During my time at university, I worked part-time at a fast-food restaurant. Most of my co-workers were students like myself, and we generally had a good work atmosphere, but there was one guy who was miserable to work with. He put in no effort, and would frequently mess up orders and be rude to customers, who would in turn complain and take their anger out on us. He was negative about everything, and his attitude dragged the mood down. When he wasn't with a customer, he would just stand around instead of helping others, so more work fell onto everyone else. When he was prompted to do something, he would always complain until he eventually, begrudgingly, did it. I hated being on shifts with him – he created situations that were bad for the team and made shifts more difficult. This in turn created a bad environment around him, and so people didn't want to work with him.

At the complete opposite end of the spectrum were three people who were incredibly fun, super helpful and always raised morale. They were the reason that I enjoyed the job on some days, and made the hard shifts bearable. We trusted and relied on each other. Be the person that raises morale, rather than the one that brings it down. It makes a huge difference, not just for yourself but for everyone you work with. You can change your environment dramatically for the better by being nice, offering people a smile, saying thank you and being grateful. Some days are always harder than others, but negativity won't make them easier, and positivity might.

WHAT'S NEXT?

No matter how many years you end up working in the industry, there will always be more to learn and new ways to develop your skills – Chapter 6 is all about finding ways to make this ongoing learning process as easy and effective as possible.

Continuous Learning

6

I've been in the industry 12-13 years, and there hasn't been a single day that I didn't learn something.

Mark Winter

The best strategy for a long-term career in game audio is to continue to learn, becoming more effective at your job by improving your skills and acquiring new ones. In this chapter, we'll delve into some strategies you can use on a daily basis to actively improve.

SEEK BETTER METRICS

If you're going to learn and grow, you need to have a way to measure your growth.

David Fairfield

If you want to get better at something, it's useful to have a way to measure yourself, allowing you to see where you are currently, and in what areas you need to improve to get to where you want to be. However, we have to be careful what metrics we use to measure ourselves, making sure that they help rather than hinder us. I often found myself feeling unhappy at the end of a work day because none of the sounds that I'd made had worked and I hadn't delivered the results that I wanted. My metric for a successful workday focused solely on the end result, and beating myself up for not achieving what I expected wasn't helpful. So, I put a notebook on my desk and wrote "Things I learned today" at the top of the page. At the end of each day, I wrote down something that I had learned that day, no matter how small, and after 2 weeks I had accumulated a bunch of lessons. With that, even difficult days felt a lot more like successes, because I knew that I was moving forward one tiny step at a time, and I had a written record of each step I took.

 DOI: 10.1201/9781003368854-7

If you have a specific goal that you want to achieve in mind, then consider the steps you can take to move towards it and measure those. Want to get better at sound design? Measure your success based on how many redesigns you do, how much feedback you've received, or how many sounds you've recorded. Want to expand your network? Create a list of conferences and events you can attend and people you can reach out to, and measure the number of lasting connections you make. Want to learn synthesis? Measure how much time you spend experimenting or how many patches and presets you've made. Whatever the goal, there are small steps you can take towards them, and identifying what they are will allow you to make measurable progress each day.

EMBRACE FAILURE

It's very easy to take an all-or-nothing approach to the challenges we face – that success is the only thing that matters – but this attitude denies us the opportunity to learn from our failures, and failures often have the most valuable lessons to teach us. If we try to do something we've never done before and it goes perfectly, how do we know that we didn't just get lucky? Did we understand what we were doing, or was it just a fluke? Try viewing challenges as opportunities to learn, regardless of whether you fail or succeed. Failure can be disheartening, but if we take the time to reflect and understand what we did wrong, we can be better prepared for similar situations in the future. This is exactly why experience is so valuable – it can't be learned, only lived.

TEACH TO LEARN

The best way to learn something is to teach it to someone else.

Sergio Ronchetti

To explain to someone how something works, you have to understand it yourself, and so teaching concepts and techniques to others is an excellent way to test and reinforce your own understanding. Before I started my game audio career, I made a video essay analysing the sound of Cuphead and demonstrated how you could recreate the game's retro soundscape. The process of learning and then explaining the techniques involved to others forced me to really engage with the processes on a deeper level, which did wonders for my own understanding. Similarly, writing this book was one big exercise in learning and teaching, refining everything I had read, watched, heard, and done down into a single text as concisely and clearly as possible. The great thing is that you don't need an audience to teach – you can do it by yourself. Try explaining something to yourself out loud, by writing it down or even producing a video explaining and demonstrating it. Could you explain it to someone else in a way they would understand?

COLLECT SOUNDS

I'm a collector of sounds, and it has changed the way I listen to the world. You can be too, by following three simple steps: Capture, Analyse and Catalogue.

- Step 1, Capture, is simply to record sounds with any device – choosing to press record forces you to listen carefully to your surroundings, both to find interesting things to record and ensure that you're able to capture them.
- Step 2, Analyse, is all about listening back to the sounds you've recorded, further testing your critical listening and helping you build a "mental encyclopaedia" of all the different sounds you've encountered.
- Finally, Step 3 is just a matter of giving your recordings suitable filenames and adding them to your collection, ready to be used in future projects. Your mental encyclopaedia will help you know when to use a sound, and a well-organised collection will make finding that sound easy.

If you're struggling to build momentum, try challenging yourself to record one sound per day for 30 days. Set a reminder on your phone and stick to it – it doesn't matter how well the sound was recorded or what it was recorded on, just that you captured it. If you're at a loss for what to record then make it a game. Write down a bunch of objects on Post-it notes and pick two at random. Use them to make sounds together and record the results. You can even pick random locations or microphone techniques if you want to. You can even invite some friends to join you, make a group chat and share your recordings with each other or post them on social media. I promise you won't regret it!

REVERSE ENGINEERING

Reverse engineering is a great way to combine theoretical research and practical application. When I was still pursuing my career as an electronic music producer, I would listen to my favourite songs and then try to recreate the synth patches I heard. Nine times out of ten I didn't come anywhere close to the original, but with each attempt, I learned something new. Slowly but surely, I built a mental map of different sounds and sound design techniques that helped me orient myself with each new attempt. The process of recreating the sound, and the things you learn through trial and error, are more important than the end result. Just like we discussed in Chapter 2, it can take time to close that gap between your vision and your ability, but with time you'll get closer and closer. Nowadays, I can get in the ballpark of the original sound fairly reliably. The time it takes to get there varies, and it always requires a lot of research, experimentation and failure, but successful or not, I'm learning something.

Experience Leads to Mastery

When Mark Winter first started working on *Insurgency*, a tactical military shooter, he had a very limited knowledge of gun sound design. He spent weeks studying the waveforms of guns from the best-sounding games, dissecting them and analysing each part of the sound. He read every interview, watched every video, and listened to every talk on the topic he could find. Slowly, he refined his process, and when the game shipped the guns sounded pretty good, but there was still a lot of room for improvement. When the game's successor *Insurgency: Sandstorm* was in development, Mark used all of his previously-collected knowledge and experience to rework the gun system from the ground up. Each gun now had multiple separate layers with different perspectives, and with the game's technological improvements new heights could be achieved. Now, with well over a decade of experience under his belt, Mark is an expert in the field of gun sound design, but he still regularly analyses the soundscapes of the newest FPS games and tries to learn wherever he can.

There are many ways you can approach reverse engineering, but just like with collecting sounds, I have a simple three-step method that helps me retain clarity during the process: Analyse, Recreate, and Iterate. I start by trying to learn as much as I can about the sound I'm trying to recreate – how does the object making the sound work from a physics standpoint? Is it mechanical, electrical and so on? What are the different elements that together create the finished sound? I try to learn as much as I can from others who have created similar sounds and have shared their knowledge on the topic in articles or talks. I also sample the sound and bring it into my DAW for analysis using tools like spectrographs and EQ, to get a better idea of what is happening at various frequencies and within the different layers of the sound.

Next, I try my best to recreate the sound using my libraries and original recorded material. In the beginning, it's important just to get the general direction right – I try to focus on the overall impression rather than the details, and instead create multiple different variations, which I then compare and contrast to find the ones that work the best. Once I have created a general "sound sketch," I start iterating and filling in the details. At this point, I can use the techniques that I learned during my analysis and put my own spin on it. Most importantly, at the end of my session, I save the DAW project and render out the different sounds I've made, so I can add them to my library for future use and reference.

POST-MORTEMS AND RETROSPECTIVES

Post-mortems (from the Latin for "after death") are a common practice in game development, in which a team comes together after a project is finished and discusses what went well, what didn't, and what could be improved going forward. The goal of this process is to take time to reflect, hear everyone's opinions, and learn from any mistakes that were made. It's an incredibly important practice, and also a popular presentation format at conferences, as it allows developers to share their experiences – and the lessons they learned – with others who could benefit from them. There is an entire YouTube playlist of GDC post-mortem talks, with well over a hundred videos dedicated to the topic.

Sometimes, a team will do a "mini post-mortem" (often referred to as a "retrospective") at the end of a milestone within an ongoing project. They are typically shorter, as they're only reviewing the last few weeks or months of work rather than years. There are plenty of different frameworks used to run these retrospectives and post-mortems. Most of them cover the same fundamental ideas but in slightly different ways. Some common frameworks include:

- Positive, Negative, Joker
- Mad, Sad, Glad
- 4 L's (Liked, Lacked, Learned, Longed for)
- KALM (Keep, Add, Less, More)

As you can probably tell, they are all very similar, and usually boil down to the same three questions: *What* worked/didn't work? *Why* did it work/not work? *How* can we make it better? To get the most out of a post-mortem or retrospective, you have to be honest with yourself and your team. Don't be overly negative, but rather praise the good, highlight the not-so-good, and give your opinion on potential ways to improve it. I would encourage you to start conducting your own post-mortems on projects that you've worked on alone. Whether that was a game you made in your spare time, a long job application process, or even a big studio upgrade, take a notebook and a pen, go to your favourite coffee shop, grab a hot beverage and reflect on how it went. The most important thing about this process is to look back at the lessons you've learned, as we often tend to jump from one task to the next without stopping, leaving plenty of valuable lessons on the road.

WHAT'S NEXT?

Our next chapter is an in-depth look at another means of continuous learning: feedback. We'll be covering what to do when asking for feedback, as well as how to give good feedback, and what to listen for when appraising someone's work.

Feedback

7

*At least half the time you have to get it wrong
before you can get it right, so let's get on with
getting it wrong. Let's get 'getting it wrong'
out of the way so we can get it right!*

Ashton Mills

I love this quote, because in my experience, the vast majority of good work I create sits atop of a mountain of bad work, and feedback is the tool that helps me reach the summit (Figure 7.1). If you are looking to learn and improve then feedback is a fantastic way to do so, as it benefits both the giver and receiver. By receiving feedback, we:

- Are able to view our work from a different perspective.
- Develop a thicker skin.
- Gain new insights and ideas that we can use in our work.

By giving feedback, we:

- Improve our critical listening and analytical skills.
- Develop our communication skills.

FIGURE 7.1 It takes a mountain of garbage to create something good.

DOI: 10.1201/9781003368854-8

- Are exposed to different styles and techniques which might inspire us in our own work.

As with any skill, we need to learn how to get the most out of it, so let's look at when and how to ask for feedback, and how to give good feedback yourself.

WHEN TO SHARE

Making a game is an inherently iterative process. In the beginning, everything is a prototype and a placeholder, from code to art to animation to audio. Over the course of development, prototypes become full features, and assets get replaced with better ones until we reach a final "shipping" quality. Because audio is the last step in the production pipeline, we need everyone else's work to be finalised before we can finish ours, but the iterative nature of game development means we often have to work with things that are unfinished or incomplete. This means we have to use concept art and our imagination to fill in the blanks.

The lesson here is to work with this iterative approach, rather than against it. Add sounds at an early stage and improve them over time with feedback from the team. I was a massive perfectionist when I first started in the industry and hated the thought of submitting work that wasn't polished, but I learned the hard way that trying to perfect something before sharing it can be a huge mistake. As we discussed in Chapter 4, the more work you do without checking in with your team, the greater the risk of having to redo or scrap everything.

Now, instead of locking myself away and working on something until it's perfect, I create a couple of initial prototype variations that I spend a limited amount of time on before reviewing them with the team. That way, I can get feedback early and eliminate the ones that don't work, leaving me to focus on the ones that do. After spending some more time refining these we go through another round of feedback, at which point we have usually eliminated all but one of the prototypes, which I can now spend a lot more time on to develop.

Crucially, this process allows your director, lead or client to not only choose the ideas they like and eliminate the ones they don't, but also to explain the reasoning behind their decisions, which will help you understand the desired outcome better. Of course, you don't always have to create multiple prototypes, but I find that creating lots of different options at an early stage can make things easier later because we've already explored our options and are less likely to wonder if something else might work at the eleventh hour.

In short, check in early and often to receive feedback – you will create better work that is more cohesive with the rest of the project if you do. Don't be afraid to share work that is in-progress – game developers spend their lives working with unfinished and placeholder assets, systems and even schedules. Everyone understands what a work in progress looks and sounds like, and to assess it based on its creative direction rather than whether it's ready to ship. I still struggle with sharing unfinished work, but the more you do it, the easier it becomes.

HOW TO SHARE

The best way to share your work is in person, as it allows the person giving feedback to listen using your setup and see your workflow in action – they can solo individual elements and make changes with you watching, which can make the process faster and smoother as there is less risk of misunderstanding. Sharing your screen with audio and video is also a good option – that way you can still ask questions and dive deeper into specific elements. If you're unable to receive feedback in real time, try sharing a video containing your work, which the person giving feedback can add a voiceover to, going through your work and offering their critiques. It allows the feedback giver to go into more depth without having to write out entire pages, and being able to hear their voice can avoid misinterpretations due to ambiguity in a written message.

In last place is written feedback, precisely because there is a lot more room for interpretation in text, which can result in misunderstandings. It can be useful sometimes, however – written feedback is great when you only need to convey some high-level ideas and nudge a person in the right direction. As with adding voiceover to a video, it also allows the feedback giver to listen in their own time and think about their answer more carefully.

Regardless of what form the feedback comes in, try to make it as easy as possible for the recipient to listen to your work – if you want someone to listen using your setup, try to have it ready to play when you ask them. This is extra important if you're asking for feedback on the internet – provide links to watch your work, rather than files people have to download. The reason is that on top of it being an extra step, workplaces often have strict policies about downloading files from the Internet, which may stop a person from being able to give feedback at all.

The Right Person For The Job

When seeking feedback, it's important that you share your work with the right people and in the right places – if you're looking for detailed feedback on a piece of music, you're better off asking a composer than an audio programmer. Consider what kind of feedback you need, and find the person who will be able to help you the most. Having a dedicated mentor is often helpful, as you can build a relationship with them and get to learn their style of feedback, making it more effective. If this isn't an option, then sharing your work in social media communities is also really effective. Some folks even do dedicated live streams offering feedback and critiques to their audiences. You can find these and other resources for feedback on the *GAL* website.

Switching Perspectives

Have you ever been really happy with a piece of work, before showing it to someone and immediately seeing all of the flaws? I certainly have, and that's a good thing, because it demonstrates the forced perspective change that occurs when you share your work. A great trick if you're stuck or feel like you've done everything you can, is exporting your work and listening back to it outside of the DAW – bonus points for listening to it on a different system like a TV or phone.

This technique is known as *referencing*, and it's incredibly useful because it allows us to listen from the perspective of someone who will be playing a game and using the speakers on their TV or laptop. By familiarising ourselves with how sounds change from one device to another, we can make sure our work sounds good across the board. When someone who isn't an audio professional gives you feedback, chances are that they will be listening to your work on a less-than-ideal setup, so bear this in mind when you ask for their feedback, and put yourself in their shoes (or rather, ears) by referencing across different devices.

ASKING FOR FEEDBACK

Whether inside or outside of work, it's important to ask for feedback kindly and respectfully, as someone is giving up their time to help you. If someone doesn't respond immediately then give them some time – they are most likely busy. It's okay to nudge them gently after a while, but give them the opportunity to decline, rather than pressuring them for a response ("Hey Greg, I sent you a redesign a week ago and just wanted to ask if you've had time to check it out, no worries if you're too busy"). If someone declines, then don't continue to ask and pressure them.

Be Specific

Asking for general feedback isn't a bad thing, but for the feedback giver, it's usually easier to focus on specific things, especially in a long clip or an entire reel. By asking questions about a specific area – for example, the Foley, or the mix – you give them something they can focus on, making it easier for them to provide useful, actionable feedback, as opposed to an overly broad "yay or nay"-type response.

Don't Overload

If you're asking someone online for feedback, send them a single clip or reel, rather than four separate ones. As I mentioned earlier, giving feedback is a task in itself, and if I see a post or message that will take up a considerable amount of time, I'm more likely to decline. If it's something shorter that won't take me a lot of time, I'll happily spend a couple of minutes sharing my thoughts.

Clarify

If you don't understand the feedback you've received, ask for clarification. It's always better to ask than to interpret. When talking to non-audio people, this can be tricky, as they often don't have the necessary vocabulary or knowledge to communicate their thoughts as effectively as a fellow audio person. In these cases, focus on trying to identify the problem from the suggested feedback, rather than asking for a solution. You can assist in this process by prompting them to talk about the emotions a soundscape should evoke, the story it should tell or the functions it should fulfil, and encourage them to use their own language rather than technical terms like EQ or compression that might be misused or misinterpreted.

Apply the Feedback

Perhaps obvious, but important: if you ask for feedback, then you should listen to and apply it. You might not always agree with it, but it's important to consider the context in which your work has to operate and experiment with the suggestions made regardless. By trying to apply the feedback, regardless of whether you stick with it or not, you respect the feedback giver's time. When I get asked to give someone feedback, only to be told after that the person is happy with their work and won't explore the suggested changes, it makes me feel like I've wasted my time.

In the workplace this is an absolute must – if your lead or director wants you to revisit your work and make adjustments then you do it, even if you end up using the original version. You will either make the work better or be able to confirm that it was right the first time, but to do that you have to experiment. Sometimes feedback can feel incredibly frustrating, especially when you're on the 4th revision and still not quite hitting the target, but spending more time with your work will allow you to learn, improve and – most importantly – understand it better, and eventually you will get there. A huge part of the feedback process is simply revisiting your work with a fresh perspective and spending more time with it.

HOW TO GIVE GOOD FEEDBACK

Broadly speaking, there are two types of feedback: general and specific. General feedback – as the name suggests – is concerned with higher-level ideas and techniques. It is "zoomed out," focused on the bigger picture, and is for identifying larger issues that are usually persistent throughout an entire piece of work. In audio, this translates to things like the artistic direction, or how well a mix makes use of the stereo field. Specific feedback – once again, as you can probably guess – is all about "zooming in" and focusing on the fine details, things like specific EQ moves on individual sounds or the balance of individual layers of a sound.

Whenever I give feedback, I start with a more general, holistic view, listening to the work in its entirety before focusing on the details. I listen and analyse, all the while taking notes, as I try to identify any areas that could be improved, and then communicate them as best I can. I think of it a bit like being a "sound doctor," examining a patient and diagnosing any problems, before prescribing a solution. Just like the retrospectives we talked about in Chapter 6, I use the questions "what, why and how" as a framework to examine the soundscape, first broadly and then again in more detail.

- *What* are we/aren't we hearing?
- *Why* are we hearing/not hearing these things?
- *How* is it impacting the soundscape?

Having analysed the work, the next step is where we deliver our "diagnosis," highlighting both the good and the bad, and making suggestions on how to fix any issues and improve the work. Once again, we can use "what, why and how" to lead us:

- *What* works well and what doesn't?
- *Why* is this the case?
- *How* can you improve on it and make it better?
- (Optional) *Why* will this help?

The guns sound really powerful, but you could **add an additional high-frequency mech layer** to help them **cut through the mix.**

I love the overall soundscape, but **the mix currently lacks clarity** because there **isn't enough contrast.** Try **raising the volume of the player's abilities and lowering the volume of ambient sounds** during key gameplay moments, to **steer the player's focus** toward the important elements.

Be Constructive

We do our best work when we feel confident and empowered.

Ashton Mills

Putting your work out there for people to critique can be scary, so it's important that the feedback we give is not only constructive but also phrased in a kind and motivating way. Constructive feedback is honest but encouraging. It recognises and compliments the good while highlighting things that could be improved, and gives suggestions on how to do so.

The Foley and character movements sound brilliant, but I feel like the environment lacks depth. By adding some additional spot FX into the scene, such as rain interacting with the different surfaces, you could bring this to the next level.

Destructive feedback does the opposite – it's discouraging, unclear and offers no help or solutions on how to improve.

The environment sounds aren't great; they need a lot more work.

Dishonest feedback can be just as devastating, giving the impression that you're on the right path only to blindside you later, and can lead to a lot of wasted time and hurt feelings.

"This sounds great, keep it up." later becoming "Sorry, we're not going to use this because it doesn't fit the direction."

Feedback is – and will always be – somewhat personal because when we care about our work, we put a little bit of ourselves into it and become attached to it. Feeling down or frustrated is completely normal when the feedback we receive is critical of something we care about; in those moments, it's best to take a step back and re-examine our work later, once we've had a chance to reflect. Knowing how feedback can affect us, it's all the more important that we be constructive and empathetic with our own criticism of others' work.

How to Start Giving Feedback

If you've just started on your game audio journey, you may feel like it's hard to contribute anything useful, and that's totally fine – everyone feels that way at first. However, I still encourage you to practise going through the framework above. Find a work to critique and type out your feedback in a document, or go old-school and use a pen and paper instead. You don't need to share it if you don't feel ready, but by actively practising each of the steps, you'll get better at and more comfortable listening critically, until you can eventually hit send on that feedback comment. Check out the resources on the *GAL* website, and have a read of the kinds of comments other people are leaving on Airwiggles – you'll soon gain an understanding of what makes feedback useful and constructive.

THE ROLE OF SOUND IN GAMES

I like to split the functions of a soundscape into three "pillars," which I use as a foundation for my analysis (Figure 7.2):
The audio should build a believable world...

- By supporting the narrative and creating an emotional response.
- Through details that bring the world to life.
- By following the audio direction to create a cohesive soundscape.

The audio should help to create a satisfying and enjoyable experience...

- By sounding appropriately powerful and responsive.
- By providing the player feedback on their actions.

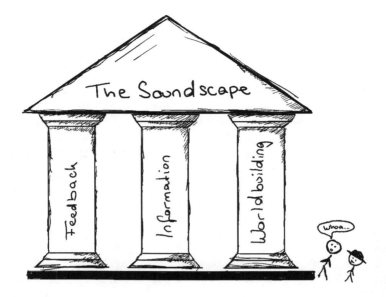

FIGURE 7.2 When giving feedback, consider these three "pillars" of analysis, and how the audio you're listening to performs in each.

The audio should give the player vital information...

- By providing clear positive and negative feedback.
- By providing spatial information.
- Through audio cues that indicate important gameplay changes.

As an example, let's take a stylised first-person shooter set in the present day and apply each of these pillars to a few elements of the weapon sounds:

Multi-layered weapons:

- The additional details make the weapons sound more believable.
- The layers create depth and movement, making the weapon satisfying to operate.
- We can alter the volume of the different layers to indicate that the player is running out of ammunition.

Hitmarkers:

- Contribute to the stylised aesthetic and art direction.
- Provide gratifying feedback when an enemy is hit.
- Indicate to the player that they have hit an enemy.

Reverb:

- Places weapons into the game space, making them feel real.
- Makes weapons feel powerful and satisfying to use, as the impulses reverberate around the space.
- Provides spatial information as to where the player is and where enemies are firing from.

Not every sound has to fulfil all three pillars all of the time, but they are a useful starting point when you're not sure if a sound fits, and can sometimes also provide us with a reason *why* a sound isn't working, as well as a solution to fix or improve it.

Steering Your Ears

In game audio, there are a lot of moving parts to keep track of, and when zooming into the details, it's easy to lose focus and miss things. We can use a "focus list" to direct our attention towards certain key areas:

- Mix – how well-balanced are the individual elements in the mix? Does the mix make full use of dynamics, the frequency spectrum and stereo field? Is the mix clear, with the important elements in focus?
- Ambience – what elements can I hear (2D ambience beds, 3D spot effects etc)? Does the ambience change to follow the camera angle and setting in a believable way?
- Foley – are the small details present (bracelets, zips etc)? Do the sounds convey an accurate sense of weight and feel? Are they synchronised properly?
- SFX – do the cadence and movement of the SFX contribute to the rhythm and feel of the piece as a whole? Are the transients cutting through the mix? Are the sounds layered, do they have depth and detail?
- "Cine" Sounds – where are they placed and what is their intended effect? How do they support or reinforce what's happening on-screen? Are they building on the scene's emotion and narrative context?

This list is fairly basic, so I encourage you to modify, remix and expand it. If you aren't a sound designer, you can still create focus lists like this for your own discipline. For example, a technical sound designer might want to assess a script's simplicity/complexity, optimisation, ease of use etc; a composer's list could examine instrumentation, emotion, pacing and so on.

Additional Tips

- When listening to a soundscape, try closing your eyes – you should still be able to get a general impression of what's happening on-screen. If not, then ask yourself why, and what needs to change for you to be able to do so.

- Our perception of frequencies changes based on their loudness, so try listening at different volumes and pay attention to how the mix changes.

- As mentioned earlier, reference the work on different systems – you will get to know how sounds are changed by the speakers they travel through, which will help you make soundscapes that sound better across the board. From laptop speakers to TV sets to gaming headsets and studio monitors, the more variety the better.

WHAT'S NEXT?

Coming up, we'll be talking about workflow, and going over ways to make your life easier by reducing friction and letting you focus on the important things.

Workflow

8

For the first couple of years in my career, I had a constant nagging thought in my head while working: "What if I'm not fast enough?" What I learned is that building speed and creative stamina largely comes down to two things: Your workspace and your approach to work. How can we make these things better? That is the central question of this chapter, and the tools that will help us make small changes that have a big impact.

WORK SMARTER

When my work colleague and I were given the task to help edit and resync the Foley for hundreds of cutscenes in a game, we knew it was going to be a lot of manual work. We needed to import the audio and video, line them up, nudge, cut or paste the clips, remove unwanted sounds and make sure it all sounded good in the end. At first, we were working at the same pace, but each day I made some small improvements, and at the end of the week I was three times faster than my counterpart.

I didn't work longer or harder, but instead smarter, figuring out how I could approach the process from a better angle, simplify it and remove or combine steps to make it fast and seamless. I batched similar processes like importing the audio and video into different projects, allowing me to get into a flow rather than stopping one task and starting another every couple of minutes. I figured out what steps could be streamlined and created custom actions in my DAW that turned many clicks into a single one – for example, adding fade-outs to multiple files in one go. I also created new keyboard shortcuts for things like skipping to the next transient to make cuts accurately, instead of using the not-so-accurate cursor, or remapping delete to a key near my pinky finger, letting me reach it without moving my entire hand each time.

Each of the improvements was incremental but together they compounded – I could now get five days' worth of work done in four, saving a full day in the process. I went on to take over the entire pipeline and make more improvements to it as I learned and encountered new problems. My philosophy was that of a lazy person – I wanted to do as little work as I needed to by making the work I did have maximum impact and efficiency. Why pedal a bicycle twice as hard when you can simply switch gears?

Remove Bottlenecks

If we take two one-litre bottles of water, cut the top off one of them, and then empty them at the exact same time, which will take longer to empty? Spoiler alert: it's the one without the bottleneck, because the narrow opening of the bottle with the top limits the rate that the water can flow (Figure 8.1).

Bottlenecks are the things responsible for slowing us down, whether that's a busy three-lane road that narrows down to a single lane, or a river obstructed by fallen debris. Our goal is to remove those bottlenecks in our lives, to make our work flow freely and easily. That way, we don't have to push through with sheer willpower but can build momentum and let the current carry us. Good work doesn't always equal hard work.

FIGURE 8.1 Which one will empty faster? 3 guesses.

Maintain Flow

You might have heard of the terms 'flow state' or being 'in the zone' used to describe the feeling of being completely immersed in a task, 'in the moment' and simply *doing*. Flow, according to psychologist Mihaly Csikszentmihalyi, can be achieved when the task has an optimal level of challenge (not too easy, not too hard), you are good at it and focused on the task itself rather than the outcome.[1] However, flow is fragile. Like a surfer riding a wave, carried by the forward momentum, it can easily be broken. When that happens, the surfer falls into the water and has to wait for the next wave and paddle to build up speed again. You might have experienced this yourself, being in the zone and working well before getting a message. You stop to look at your phone, and then when you try to get back to work the feeling has already slipped away. Now, you have to use your own willpower to push through the task and build up speed from zero again.

Distractions not only throw us off our metaphorical surfboards, but if enough of them are present, they will also kill the waves, preventing us from building momentum at all. The most fundamental and basic thing you can do to improve your workflow and stay on that surfboard is to remove distractions. This will allow you to do what Cal Newport calls "deep work," doing more things in less time and to a better standard than if you were working in a distracted environment.[2] The beauty is that if you incorporate regular, distraction-free work into your day, you will have more time to take breaks, relax and do other things like play video games.

In a conversation with David Fairfield about the topic, he illustrated it like this:

> Imagine a child in a room with a pen and paper, and a task to fill out the paper. How would they do in a distraction-free environment? Now imagine another room, but this time next to the pen and paper there are twenty cool toys all moving and making sounds. How would the child do this time?

I love YouTube – when I open it, I'm greeted with a curated feed of videos that match my exact current interests – but that also makes it the mother of all distractions. The best way not to get distracted by the toys is not to give distractions a chance, so I do the following:

I isolate myself virtually and physically.

- Virtually by putting my phone face-down on silent, closing all non-work-related browser tabs, not opening new tabs and turning off notifications. The tabs I can't close go on a separate virtual desktop that I have to manually switch to. I press F11 to make that tab or program full-screen to hide everything else and fully immerse myself in whatever task I'm doing.

- Physically by closing doors, windows and maybe even curtains or blinds.

I commit to a timeframe.

- I set a start time so I can prepare myself and my space for when I start working – I find that the early mornings or late evenings, when there is no one around to bother you, are great times that can be carved out for deep work.
- I set an end time, to avoid overworking myself and allowing me to feel comfortable committing fully to deep working, knowing that I can ease off the gas a little when the clock runs out.

Micro vs Macro

When it comes to our workflows, we can distinguish between bottlenecks at a micro or macro scale. Micro bottlenecks happen in our moment-to-moment workflow, like having to get your guitar out of its case each time you want to play or setting up a new project in your DAW each morning instead of using a template. Macro-level bottlenecks affect us on an hour-to-hour and day-to-day basis, like having a slow computer, outdated and bug-prone software or bad communication with the team.

Micro-level bottlenecks are usually easy to fix. To use our river analogy from earlier, they are small pieces of debris, and we increase the flow with each one we remove. Macro bottlenecks, on the other hand, are much larger and often require more time and resources to remove. However, instead of bringing in a crane and dragging away the entire piece of debris at once, which is costly and time-consuming, we can simply break it down into smaller chunks and remove them one by one. Applying our "little monsters" idea from Chapter 2, we can turn a single macro-level problem into several smaller, micro-level problems that are more easily dealt with (Figure 8.2).

You can only fix a problem once you become aware of it, of course, and you do that by examining your processes.

- Problem/Action – What is the main issue or action to be streamlined?
- Observe – What is the process? What are the steps involved?
- Identify – What are the things causing friction? Where are bottle-necks being created?
- Improve – What can I do to reduce friction and remove bottlenecks?

FIGURE 8.2 Make little monsters out of big monsters, and daunting tasks become far more manageable.

Example 1

Problem – My computer is slow

Observe – The key components affecting my computer's speed are the CPU, GPU and RAM. The amount of storage space I have available, and the overall health of my operating system are also factors.

Identify – I don't have enough RAM, and my computer is struggling to run all the programs I need to simultaneously.

Improve – Save money to purchase more/upgraded RAM.

Example 2

Problem – Levels are slow to load.

Observe – The steps to load a level are: download the latest build, open the game engine, open the level, and wait for the shaders to compile.

Identify – Shader compilation is the slowest step.

Improve – Ensure that the latest build is downloaded the night before; write a list of other jobs you can do while waiting (recording, research, writing documentation, etc.); prioritise doing all the work for one level in a single sitting, rather than switching back and forth between levels.

Example 3

Action – Pressing the Delete key.

Observe – I have to move my hand away from its normal position to press the key.

Identify – Having to move my entire hand back and forth is slower than pressing a nearby key.

Improve – Remap the delete function to another key that's more easily reachable.

Example 4

Action – Adding a low-pass filter to a track.

Observe – The steps are: select the track, open the plugin selection menu, search for an EQ plugin, load the EQ and add a low-pass filter to the EQ.

Identify – This process can be automated.

Improve – Create an EQ preset for a low-pass filter and assign a keyboard shortcut to load it on a track.

As you can see, even the simplest of actions can be streamlined and made easier – it's all about making the process of realising your ideas as frictionless as possible. Try applying this framework to some aspects of your workflow – what actions can you automate? What are the major obstacles slowing you down?

Modify Your Tools

Modifying your tools is similar to modding a game – you add something to improve the experience, whether that is making the game look better, run smoother, sound cooler, or simply be more fun. I used to play a lot of Minecraft, and a huge part of it for me was the mods – from fancy shaders and new game modes to additional item slots, they were a way to personalise the game and make it more fun. Mods don't have to be big or complicated, however. In fact, they are usually all about small details and quality-of-life improvements.

Today, I apply this same philosophy of personalisation to all of my tools. We've already talked about custom actions, remapping and keyboard shortcuts. Most DAWs have the capability to create new keyboard shortcuts, and some even have macros or custom actions that allow you to chain keyboard commands together in sequence and activate them with a single button. Even superficial or non-functional changes like changing the colour scheme or UI layout of a program can go a long way toward making it easier to use.

I encourage you to do some homework on your DAW, game engine or integrated development environment of choice and find out how you can customise them to do the things you need in the way you want. The same goes for hardware and even your whole workspace. Quality generic tools are good, but quality custom tools are better – don't be shy to put your own touch on things, whether that's remapping key commands, adding a quick-release microphone clip to your rig, or building customised storage for your gear.

Design Your Space

I've spent my entire professional game audio career (so far) working, sleeping and living in the same room. In that time, it's been through countless iterations as I change and adapt it to suit my needs. I live by the philosophy that your space needs to evolve and grow with you – in other words, it's always a work in progress.

I have a vision of my dream creative space, but it changes with my interests. I used to want a huge studio with a cinema screen in a dark space like one of those film mixing stages. Then I started getting more into Foley, and the thought of a warehouse studio with lots of props and various Foley pits sounded much cooler. Eventually, I got really into DIY and building small things, so now I've added a workshop to my wish list. My current space looks nothing like any of these visions. However, the things I've acquired and the way I've set the space up still reflect those interests and work towards these visions using the space and gear that I've got.

By creating makeshift Foley pits out of cardboard boxes padded out with clothes to dampen the sound and collecting a few boxes of props, I now have a lightweight Foley setup. I don't have a full workshop yet, but I acquired a couple of tools and bought a keyboard tray so that my desk is empty, allowing me to use it to build things. In addition, I've created a little recording nook, using some acoustic panels and carpet to create an acoustically treated space, which allows me to set up my mics and record props easily.

It's not perfect but it's functional, and getting better with each upgrade. Like everything else that we've talked about in this book, we shouldn't be aiming for perfection, but for consistent improvement. That being said, there are some techniques and tactics you can employ to design your space to your needs and make the best of what you've got.

HOW TO CREATE A WORKSPACE

When we design our workspace, there are three pillars that are useful to keep in mind to help inform your decisions about the space:

- Function – what is the purpose of the space?
- Flow – how can it help me work effortlessly?
- Feeling – how do I want it to make me feel?

Our end goal is to design a space that fulfils our needs, allows us to do good work easily, and feels good to be in. Let's examine each of the pillars in more depth and then apply the principles in practice.

Function – Purpose of Space

Our first pillar is fairly simple: what do I want to do in this space? In general, the more functions a space needs to fulfil, the less functional it becomes – if your workspace is also your living room, bedroom and dining room, then it probably won't be the best workspace it can be. However, like many others (myself included), you might find yourself in exactly that situation, in which case one of the things you can do is try to separate your space into smaller, specialised areas. I've split my room into a workspace that needs to accommodate my job and creative hobbies, and a rest space where I play games, sleep, relax and get dressed. This separation helps me to optimise both spaces for their primary functions.

Space – Workspace.
Functions – Designing sounds, recording audio and video.
Needs – Good lighting and acoustics, speakers, computer, recording space, audio and video equipment.

Space – Rest space.
Functions – Relaxing, gaming, sleeping and getting dressed.
Needs – Bed/sofa, TV, games console(s), clothes and mood lighting.

Separating these areas from one another physically can also help, either through some tactical furniture arranging or just putting up a screen door to keep your workspace separated from your living space. The more distinction between spaces, the easier it is to tailor them to your needs individually. Conversely, when it comes to the things *in* our spaces, the opposite is true – the more uses they have, the better, especially in smaller spaces where things become cluttered quickly. This applies to our tools, but also to things like furniture - a clothes rack makes for an effective piece of DIY acoustic treatment.

Flow – Effortless Work

The goal of this pillar is to make your workflow as seamless as possible by setting up your space in a way that minimises friction and maximises ease of use – how can I do the things I want to do effortlessly? We already covered some of the steps of this pillar earlier in the chapter, namely analysing your workflow and identifying and removing bottlenecks, but when it comes to the design of the space itself, there are some additional rules of thumb that I find make my life a lot easier.

Everything in Its Place

Each item you own should have a place it can call home – somewhere that you know it lives and can always be found when you need it. When you're finished with an item, or at the end of the work day, everything goes back in its place, ensuring your space stays tidy and things don't go missing. Try to group similar things together such as recording gear or important documents. That way, if you can't remember exactly where something is, you'll know roughly where to look. Label things like boxes, folders and cables (especially power leads), so you don't have to start opening boxes to know what's inside, or unplug random cables to see what they're connected to.

Exactly where things should live will depend on what space you use them in and how often you need them. Ideally, things you use while at your desk should be within reach without leaving your chair and not under your bed. As always, experimentation and iteration are key – try new ideas, and don't be afraid to move things around as your needs dictate. If you're struggling to find a suitable home for something, ask yourself how essential it is. Do you need more storage, or are there things taking up space that you don't need? 'Everything in its place' is not just about where you keep things, but what things you keep.

Remember: Home improvements take time. Set aside half a day or so every couple of months to make changes and fixes. Whether updating plugins and adding new keyboard shortcuts or tightening the loose screw on your office chair, these smaller tasks accumulate quickly. I often procrastinate until there are a bunch, then batch them together and do them all at once. Use whatever strategy works for you, but make time to work on the list and keep it from getting overwhelming.

Feeling – The Vibe

Your environment has a big impact on your productivity and health, so this pillar is all about how you can transform your functional workspace into a creative space that enhances your wellbeing. How can I make it feel good to spend my time here?

Think about your five senses – sight, smell, taste, touch and hearing – and how well your workspace satisfies those senses:

- Is your space lit properly? Do you have natural light or artificial; is your screen too bright or too dark?
- Does your room smell nice? Is it well-ventilated?
- Do you have food available to keep you going while you're working? Are you eating healthy snacks or junk?
- Is your chair comfortable? Is the temperature of the room suitable to work in?
- Is your workspace quiet (apart from the noise you're making, of course)? Are there any unwanted acoustic noises or resonances in the space?

This is far from an exhaustive list of questions, but you get the idea. In order to work well, we need to be comfortable and not trapped in a stuffy room with a creaky chair and no blinds. If you're working in an office then some decisions are made for you or have to be made with your co-workers in mind (the aircon temperature will be an eternal battle), but if you're working from home then you're free to do whatever you need to make the space work for you.

Once you've made the space fit for habitation, you can start making it your own by decorating it with things that bring some creativity and joy to it – photos, Lego sets, instruments, a bubble gum dispenser, whatever makes it *your* space. Some personal touches can even serve practical functions too, like hanging up rugs and carpets to act as DIY acoustic treatment or houseplants to help keep the air fresh.

RETAIL THERAPY

One of the joys of audio technology is that there is an endless supply of cool and interesting tools to play around with. The downside is that it's easy to fall into the habit of buying gear that you want but don't actually need, colloquially known as "Gear Acquisition Syndrome," or *GAS*. Buying new tools is not a bad thing inherently, but trying to spend your way out of creative or technical problems is. So how can we avoid GAS and make smart, guilt-free purchases without breaking the bank?

Be Patient

One of the best ways to know whether you actually need something is to wait. It's easy to buy something impulsively and justify it afterwards, but the pull of a shiny new product becomes a lot less strong the longer we wait. Give it a week or two before you buy that new tool, and if you still feel like it's essential, then go for it!

Find It Pre-Loved

Buying and unboxing a brand-new piece of gear is exciting, but it comes at a high price and has an impact on the environment. Buying second-hand can be a fantastic way to save money and help the environment by giving something a new home. There are plenty of places to shop for second-hand gear, from generalist sites like eBay and Facebook Marketplace to specialised audio ones like Reverb and Audio Gold, with everything you could ever need (and everything you don't!) available for sale.

Stick to a Budget

A side effect of GAS is that you might find yourself with a cool modular synth, but not enough money for rent or food. Managing money is tricky, but one method I find helpful is to set up a savings account for buying gear, diverting a small percentage of your income there each month. Any money in this account can be used to buy whatever you want. Doing this will also force you to wait while you save up, giving you time to assess whether you really need something.

Rent or Borrow

Sometimes, you need a very specific piece of gear for a very specific task, which might only come up once a year. Instead of purchasing that gear, try asking around to see if someone local to you might have it already and be willing to lend it to you. If you don't use gear often, it may be cheaper (or even free, if you're lucky) to rent when you need it instead of buying your own.

WHAT'S NEXT?

Our next chapter is all about problem-solving – what to expect, how to fix things when they go wrong, and how to prevent things from going wrong again, or even at all.

REFERENCES

1. Csikszentmihalyi, M. (1975) *Beyond Boredom and Anxiety.* San Francisco, CA: Jossey-Bass.
2. Newport, C. (2015) *Deep Work: Rules for Focused Success in a Distracted World.* New York City, NY: Grand Central Publishing.

"Houston, We Have A Problem" **9**

TYPES OF PROBLEM

Problems are everywhere, and no matter what discipline you work in you will spend considerable time battling with them. However, we tend to invest very little time into learning *how* to approach, solve and - most importantly – prevent problems in creative and effective ways. In game audio, we can organise problems roughly into three categories:

Technical Problems (Aka Bugs)

Technical problems are generally the kind that occur due to errors in the middleware, game engine or code, which we refer to as bugs. They typically happen at an implementation level, causing audio playback to break in various ways, such as:

- A sound not being triggered, resulting in silence.
- A sound being triggered too often, causing multiple instances of the sound to overlap.
- A variable in game data that is needed to modify the audio being broken or incorrect.
- An empty sound file being implemented, resulting in a missing sound (oops).

Auditory Problems

Auditory problems are the kind we encounter when things just don't sound "right." The game might be failing to convey information, feedback and emotion

DOI: 10.1201/9781003368854-10

to the player effectively, or something might just sound bad for whatever reason. The solutions to auditory problems can come in many different forms, from technical tweaks to implementation or mixing, to artistic tweaks like modifying or changing a sound that doesn't fit the creative direction. Examples include:

- It's unclear to the player when they are running out of ammunition.
- The car doesn't feel fast enough when driving at high speeds.
- The level in this horror game doesn't feel scary.
- There's too much going on at once when there are lots of enemies on-screen.

Pipeline Problems

Sometimes, there are problems with the way a project is being managed that need to be fixed in order for us to do our best work. These are logistical and interpersonal problems affecting the everyday processes and systems that we create and use in the workplace. Examples include:

- Animation timings keep changing, and the audio team isn't being made aware of the changes, only finding them in retrospect.
- A regularly scheduled meeting with no clear purpose or objectives, wasting development time instead of saving it.
- The delivery speed of assets varies drastically between team members doing the same thing.
- A key member of the team leaving or taking extended time off.

SOLVING PROBLEMS

Every problem will require slightly different things from you to solve, but the general approach remains the same: reproduce, debug, fix and test.

Reproduce

Being able to reliably recreate a problem is an important part of identifying the root cause and fixing it. If a sound isn't playing back half the time, it's going to be a lot harder to pinpoint the cause than if it weren't playing at all, so step one is getting the problem to happen 100% of the time. In game development, this is often handled by quality assurance testers, or QA testers for short, whose role is dedicated to finding bugs and figuring out how to reproduce them as reliably as possible – *what* happens, *when* and *where*. The bugs, as well as the steps to reproduce them, are reported to the development team, who can then set about identifying *why* they happen.

While QA testers are focused primarily on finding and reproducing technical problems, the same "what, when and where" metric can be applied to auditory and pipeline problems too – identifying the cause of pipeline problems is usually less about reproducing the issue, as they are likely to be larger-scale, systemic problems, but it's still important to build as clear a picture of the issue as we can. Take a look back at the example problems from earlier, and try applying this framework to them. Some problems may not have an answer to all three questions; some may have multiple answers.

Debug

Once we can reproduce a problem, we can start asking *why* it's happening. This is often the hardest part of the process, but there are some things we can do to make it easier, first and foremost being: Don't make assumptions – sometimes the answer is hiding in plain sight (Figure 9.1).

FIGURE 9.1   No answer is too obvious; sometimes problems are really that simple.

"There's no way *that's* causing the problem" is a sentence that has wasted countless hours of my time, spent looking for the cause of a problem that was right in front of me. Once, while I was working on a game, I heard some duplicated dialogue playing in a cutscene. Naturally, I checked the dialogue events in my middleware and in the game engine, and they were fine. I soloed the sound effects, the "cine" sounds, the music and even the ambience, but the duplicate dialogue was nowhere to be found.

On that project, I was responsible for the Foley pipeline, so I had been implementing most of the Foley myself. I hadn't checked the Foley because there was no way it could have been in there. You can guess what happened next, can't you? Sure enough, the dialogue had been rendered into the Foley stem for the cutscene, causing the doubling effect. Much like how step one of computer troubleshooting is turning it off and on again, and that often manages to fix the problem, we have to be careful not to dismiss an explanation for appearing too simple or obvious.

Ask the Right Questions

It's important to make sure that we consider problems from a "zoomed-out" point of view and avoid fixating on details that might not need changing. For example, a piece of feedback you might receive while working on a racing game is "the car doesn't sound fast enough." This sentence makes us focus on the car and brings to mind solutions like changing the engine sound or the tyre noise, but we've unwittingly zoomed in too far to see

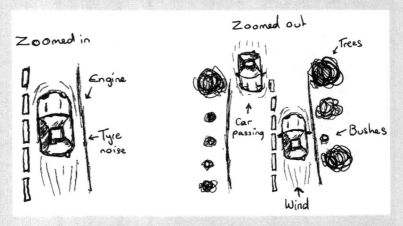

FIGURE 9.2 If we fixate too much on one element of a scene, we lose sight of the context in which that element exists.

the problem clearly. When we ask, "why does it not sound fast enough?" we need to ask another question: "what does moving at high speed sound like?" This additional question brings our focus back to the problem and allows us to consider it from all angles. Maybe the car sounds are fine, and we need to make changes to other things like the wind or the sounds of lamp posts and trees flying past (Figure 9.2).

Rubber Duck Debugging

Have you ever gone to ask a question and then realised the answer as you're explaining the problem to someone? I have, many times, and it turns out that there is a reason for this – when we explain a problem that we are having to someone, talking them through it step by step, we are forced to clarify our thoughts and articulate them in a way that the listener can understand. By doing this, we inadvertently improve our own understanding of the problem, and sometimes that allows us to see the answer for ourselves – teaching to learn, just like we discussed in Chapter 6.

The great thing about this is that you don't need to talk to another person to make use of this process. The name "Rubber Duck Debugging" was coined by Andrew Hunt and David Thomas, who chose the little yellow bathtub companion as their audience stand-in, but obviously, any inanimate object will do – they're all equally good listeners.[1] Of course, sharing your problems with other people or communities like Airwiggles (so long as you're not breaking any NDAs) is also a good idea, as someone else might have experience with the same issue and know what the cause is – they may even have a solution to it as well.

On top of verbal processing, I find it helpful to engage even more of my senses by writing information down on Post-it notes and sometimes even illustrating it through basic diagrams and drawings. That way I don't have to hold all the information in my head and can examine the problem and all of its individual components from different angles.

Profilers and Debug Logs

Sometimes, you need more information than what is available at first glance to get to the root of a problem. That's where profilers and debug logs come in to save the day. A profiler is a tool that shows us the journey a sound file takes from the middleware to the game engine and out of the speakers. This allows us to see exactly what events start and stop playback of the sound, what additional processing is happening to the sound (such as reverb or filtering for distant effects), as well as the raw values of the game data affecting these processes (the distance as a number). All of this helps us pinpoint the exact reason why things are going wrong.

Whenever I encounter a bug that I can't solve and ask my technical sound designer for help, the first thing he will ask me is if I've checked the profiler. Now, I always make sure to check it before I go to him and give him a summary of my findings. If the journey from the middleware to the audio output is smooth then the bug is probably happening somewhere in the game engine, in which case we need to dive into even more technical waters. That's where the debug log – also known as a console or output log – comes into play, with error messages and logs that often contain further clues. From there, we have to follow the breadcrumb trail and potentially dive into the game engine's documentation or consult the Internet. You can find a detailed look at profilers and debug logs on the *GAL* website.

Fix and Test

Once we've diagnosed the problem and found our "what, when, where and why," we can use this information to create and test a potential solution. Some problems practically solve themselves once we know what's wrong – this is usually the case for bugs, where problems can be caused by missing files or mistakes in code formatting – but some are a lot more complex and may require several things to be changed or implemented in order to fix. This is often the case with auditory or pipeline problems, where issues are more likely to be the result of conflicts between multiple systems or ideas. In these instances, it's useful to take a moment to consider all of the different possible solutions, the pros and cons of each, and what knock-on effects your solutions might have on other systems – you don't want to create more headaches for yourself further down the road.

Regardless of whether it's a problem that can be solved with one change or many, it can be a good idea to see if there are other games that have encountered and dealt with similar problems in the past, and if so, how they solved them. Take the auditory problem we mentioned earlier: communicating to the player in a first-person shooter that they are running out of ammunition. This is a common situation in many games, and so various solutions have been developed over the years, from UI sound alerts, to character dialogue, to changing the sound of the weapons themselves as their ammo count decreases.

Each of these solutions has its pros and cons – is the feedback clear enough? Is it likely to grow annoying with repetition? Which solutions are less work to implement than others? How easy would it be to apply this solution to all of the game's weapons? Identifying the upsides and downsides of each idea makes it easier to determine which will work best in a given situation, or if a combination of different ideas can help manage the negative effects that one solution alone would cause.

With your solution(s) chosen, you can start figuring out the steps you need to take in order to put them into practice. That might mean asking programmers or technical sound designers for access to additional game data, creating new sounds to accompany or replace existing ones, or reassigning jobs within your team to balance the workload more effectively. Since pipeline problems affect multiple people – sometimes the entire development team – it's important that we communicate our proposed solutions clearly and explain the reasoning behind them. Sometimes, the limiting factor when solving pipeline issues is feasibility, having to find a suitable compromise between how other people work and what they're able or willing to do differently.

With your changes made, try and reproduce the problem again – is everything working as expected now? Have any new problems appeared? It might take time for some changes to have a noticeable effect, especially ones relating to pipeline and production issues, but it's important to monitor changes to ensure that they're not doing more harm than good. Like everything in gamedev, troubleshooting is an iterative process, so don't be afraid to make further changes or even scrap them and return to a previous idea.

What If I Get Stuck and Can't Solve a Problem?

Sometimes, we just can't figure something out, no matter how much we talk to our rubber duck. In those moments, don't be afraid to reach out and ask for help, be that from a co-worker, your project lead, or even friends and acquaintances from outside of work (though, of course, make sure you don't break any NDAs in doing so). There's no shame in asking for help!

The more I do the job, the more I realise how much I don't know.

Jake Gaule

Practising Problem-Solving

When it comes to actively getting better at problem-solving, especially bug-fixing, programming is one of the most effective ways to improve. It requires you to take a logical, step-by-step approach as you're writing instructions for the computer that it will interpret literally. If you miss any steps, the computer can't fill in the blanks for you – the program will simply fail. When these failures happen, you can go through each step of the problem-solving process, reproducing, identifying, fixing and then testing.

I'm not suggesting that you do a computer science degree in your spare time, but rather set a goal of creating a simple game or other piece of media that tests your skills. I taught myself in this way, building a simple platformer in Unity using C#. I had a list of functions I wanted to implement – player movement, jumping, moving platforms, interactive music – and with the help of a few friends and forums on the Internet, I was able to make it happen.

I highly recommend that you try it yourself – engines like Unity, Unreal or Godot are free to use for beginners and even small businesses in some cases. Think up a basic concept, or try to recreate a classic game like *Tetris* or *Breakout*. Don't worry about original assets or music; focus on the programming and use the myriad of free assets available on your engine of choice – this is what they're for! It will be a challenge, but you'll learn an incredible amount about game development and problem-solving, and the finished game will be perfect for your demo portfolio!

PREVENTING PROBLEMS

Preventing problems from happening is always more effective than fighting them, so it's important that we think ahead whenever possible and consider the long-term impact of our actions and decisions. But how do we measure our success in preventing problems, and what does prevention even look like? It's easy to measure our success in fixing a load of bugs, but it's a lot harder to quantify the things that *didn't* happen because of our work.

A lot of the time, preventing problems is all about having contingencies in place that can solve or negate them before they arise. Figuring out what these contingencies need to be can be done by examining a current or past problem, or by looking ahead for hypothetical future problems. Let's look at an example of a pipeline problem: a senior member of the team has left the company, leaving a large knowledge gap that needs to be filled. To get to the bottom of the problem we can simply ask *why* until we reach the core of the issue.

Why is there a knowledge gap? Because someone left.
Why did this create a knowledge gap? Because their knowledge wasn't documented anywhere.
Why wasn't it documented? Because there's no process for doing so.
Why is there no process? Because no one had considered what would happen if someone left.

With that, we have our core problem – team members' knowledge is not being documented well enough – and can begin solving it in whatever way is deemed most appropriate:

- Train staff to a higher level across the board, so that no one person is solely responsible for a task.
- Create and maintain a "company wiki" with all the necessary information that workers can refer to.

With cases like this, where we're examining a current or past problem, putting contingencies in place can be relatively simple once the source of the problem is found. The challenge is being able to anticipate problems before they manifest. Where do we start with preventing issues that haven't appeared yet? According to the Pareto Principle (also known as the 80/20 rule), around 80% of problems stem from only 20% of causes.[2] These are the "vital few" that create the most issues for us and therefore should be the main focus of our prevention efforts. Here are some of the best prevention efforts I've identified over the course of my career (so far) that'll help keep those 20% causes from creating 80% problems.

Technical Problems

One of the technical challenges of game audio is getting all of the different systems we use to play nicely with each other. When it comes to the fundamentals of the engine, that's largely out of your hands, but everything you build on top of the foundational elements needs to be reliable and stable. Hacking together something that does the job might be quick in the short term, but the more unstable pieces you stack on top of one another, the more unsteady the whole becomes, and the greater the fallout when something does finally break.

Things don't have to work the first time – mistakes will happen, and there's no shame in that – but you have to take responsibility for making it work properly. Test things before you submit them to ensure that your changes don't break something else. Use placeholders if you don't have the finished assets yet to make sure that you're not leaving any landmines for anyone else by submitting incomplete work. Get a colleague or friend to review your work too, if you can! A rubber duck is great for getting things done alone, but when contributing to a larger group's work it pays to have another pair of eyes check your work for any errors you've missed.

Auditory Problems

For auditory problems, the biggest cause is usually that people forget about the core functions that their sounds need to fulfil: Building a believable world, providing feedback, and conveying information to the player. Just like we covered in Chapter 7, each piece of audio has a role to play in games, and the key to avoiding auditory issues is to keep those roles in mind. Create a plan for the game's audio direction, if you don't already have one, and let it inform the work you do and the decisions you make.

Find references and examples from other games, movies, TV shows, whatever matches the vision that you or your team has for the project, and treat them as a point of comparison for your own work. This is doubly important if you're one of a team of sound designers, where the creative direction becomes the standard to which everyone's work needs to conform, regardless of personal style. Most importantly, as we've covered plenty already, get feedback early and often - the sooner you check in, the sooner you can make corrections if you've strayed from the intended vision.

Pipeline Problems

Avoiding pipeline problems is all about having clear and well-thought-out processes in place for everything from how meetings are conducted (having a host rather than a free-for-all) to what software is used and how file-names are formatted. The key to ensuring that everything works properly and everyone is on the same page? *Communication.* Game development requires people from different disciplines to all work together, and each person's work is dependent on someone else's. If we don't communicate effectively with everyone else, misunderstandings and unintended conflicts will pop up unexpectedly, as someone changes an animation without telling audio that they need to re-synchronise the Foley. Establish a regular dialogue with other departments and keep each other informed of decisions that may impact one another.

Since pipeline problems are often larger-scale logistical issues, planning ahead – and ensuring that you ask the right questions – is vital. Are you going to rent equipment and record the vehicle sounds you need, or buy a library and adapt it to suit? How often are you going to check in with other teams to ensure everybody stays up to date? You don't have to be the team lead to think about these bigger-picture issues, either anticipating problems or examining them post-mortem. Pipeline problems are everyone's problems, and so finding effective solutions benefits everyone, too.

WHY PROBLEMS ARE ACTUALLY GOOD

We tend to view problems as a purely negative thing, and understandably so – problems usually mean more work trying to fix them – but as my first boss once told me, "You learn more on a bad day than on any good day." Five years and a lot of bad days later, I can confirm that he wasn't wrong. Learning to manage and overcome problems has been a vital experience, helping me build my "Frustrationstoleranz," as we say in German. This resilience in the face of setbacks is not just valuable at work, but also in our daily lives, improving our ability to handle stressful situations and roll with the punches. As the saying goes, be like water and allow yourself to adapt to the ever-changing world we live in.

WHAT'S NEXT?

In Chapter 10, we'll be talking about "creative stamina," and how to find inspiration and motivation on those days when nothing comes to you easily.

REFERENCES

1. Hunt, A. and Thomas, D. (1999) *The Pragmatic Programmer.* Boston, MA: Addison-Wesley.
2. Dunford, R., Su, Q. and Tamang, E. (2014) 'The Pareto Principle', *The Plymouth Student Scientist*, 7(1), pp. 140–48. Available at: http://hdl.handle. net/10026.1/14054 (Accessed 21 January 2024).

Creative On Demand

10

Working in game audio can be a creatively rewarding experience, as we get to make exciting and evocative pieces of art every day. Some days, however, it feels more like we *have* to make exciting art, even when we're not feeling it – we have to be "creative on demand." This is especially true if you're employed full-time by a company – you're expected to show up, turn on your computer and spend the day creating, regardless of how you're feeling. We all have days when we run out of stamina or simply don't know where to start – I still have some days like this, but over time I've managed to improve my creative stamina and found techniques that help me get into the flow. I believe that we require two things in order to be creative on demand:

- Inspiration – outside influences that get our creative juices flowing.
- Motivation – intrinsic and extrinsic factors that give us that initial push to start working and build the momentum to keep going.

Creative work doesn't just happen in front of the computer – it can happen anywhere, anytime. I've had some of my biggest creative breakthroughs in my job away from my desk, on a walk to the grocery store, on the toilet, or in the shower. The awesome thing about creativity is that you don't need anything except your imagination to come up with new ideas or solve problems. Often, the key is to switch perspective by stepping away from a problem and looking at it from afar, but more on that later.

INSPIRATION

Have you ever come away from an activity or conversation that left you inspired, enthusiastic, and yearning to create something? I have many times, and every time I encounter an activity that gets me into that state of inspiration, I try to take note of it physically or mentally. By doing this, I've built a

 DOI: 10.1201/9781003368854-11

list of things that I can rely on to put me in a creative state if I ever need an extra injection of inspiration. For me, these include:

- Going field recording.
- Taking walks in nature.
- Using new or different tools.
- Learning a new sound design technique.
- Watching a movie/show with amazing sound.
- Listening to other people's sound design work.
- Playing video games with beautiful soundscapes.
- Experimenting without a goal in mind (sound doodles).
- Watching sound design breakdown videos on YouTube.
- Having conversations with other people about game audio.
- Reading an article/blog post about the soundscape of a cool game.

> **Task – What Inspires You?**
>
> Have a think, and write your own list of things that inspire you. Chances are we'll have a few activities in common, as well as some unique to you. Just like when we talked about "filling the hopper" in Chapter 2, they can be specific to game audio or completely unrelated - whatever makes you feel creative.

Motivation

Now that you are inspired and ready to tackle creative problems, it's time to actually sit down and do the work. Usually, the hardest part is simply getting started – when riding a bike on flat ground, getting yourself moving requires the most energy; once you're in motion, it's much easier to maintain. Here, the thing that helps us get started is *motivation* – the discipline and willpower to close our five browser tabs, open the DAW and stop procrastinating. Motivation seems to come and go sporadically, and relying on waking up feeling motivated is unlikely to get us far, so it's important that we prepare for those off days and have things ready to help push us along, just as we did with our inspiration list.

Reason

For me, the first thing that I need to feel motivated is a good reason to do something. Obviously, most work comes with the standard reason of "I need to pay rent and eat food", but valid as that is, it's not super compelling when we're struggling to feel creative. Try viewing tasks as opportunities to do something you'd been meaning to do anyway – a sound design task is an opportunity to experiment with a new plugin, someone asking for feedback is a chance to practise your critical listening, and so on.

Pressure

> If you give yourself six weeks to design a sound, it'll take six weeks.
>
> *Jake Gaule*

When there's no urgency to do something, I tend to procrastinate. To combat this, I set myself arbitrary deadlines for tasks, adding time pressure and creating a sense of urgency, which kickstarts my motivation. I do this with all of my creative endeavours, like when I made the *Game Audio Learning* website. As an independent project, there was theoretically no deadline at all until I set one, and to make it real, I told a bunch of my friends about it, who could hold me accountable for meeting it.

Creating these kinds of artificial deadlines can be useful even when you have an existing deadline to work to. If you've been given eight weeks to complete a job, giving yourself a six-week deadline gives you a spare two weeks at the end of the process for refining or troubleshooting your work. Of course, it's important that you avoid overworking yourself with unrealistic deadlines – this should be a tool to make your life easier, not harder.

Progress

It's easy to motivate yourself for a short sprint or a single task, but a lot harder to stay motivated for a whole marathon or long project. What do you do once the novelty and excitement of doing something new wears off, and you have to stick at it?

A way that I find useful personally is to track my accomplishments as much as I can. Using our framework from Chapter 2, I make little monsters out of big monsters and write all of my subtasks on Post-it notes – one note might contain four subtasks that I cut into pieces. I pin these pieces to a wall, and once I complete a task, I put the relevant piece into a little container. At the end of each month, I have a little pile of ripped Post-it notes that show me how much I've achieved, which motivates me to continue working.

Sometimes, a lack of motivation can stem from being unsure of our abilities. In these situations, looking back at old projects, listening to a song you wrote a long time ago or checking out the blueprint for a system that you designed, is a fantastic way to reinvigorate your motivation by seeing how far you've come. Sometimes, progress is not necessarily what you've achieved, but rather what you've learned and how you're improving.

Remove Hurdles

This is essentially a combination of two lessons we've covered previously: Make it easy and work smarter. The more steps between you and the ability to create, the harder it is to summon the energy to start, so give yourself shortcuts – create a template project for your DAW with a track armed and ready to record; create macros and scripts that streamline repetitive tasks for you. The less friction we have to overcome as we work, the easier it is to be creative.

> **Task – What's Getting In Your Way?**
>
> Think about the things that stop you from getting started on a task – are there obstacles getting in the way when you try to work? If so, what steps can you take to remove them or reduce their impact? Similarly, what are the tasks that you find uninteresting, and how can you make them more engaging or rewarding?

HOW TO BUILD CREATIVE STAMINA

Creativity is a muscle that you can train – the more you use it and put it under strain, the stronger it will get. Like strength training, consistent, regular repetition of exercise is the best way to improve. That means challenging yourself to daily practice and – crucially – doing things that you have never done before, or that you are less good at. In order for growth to happen and your creative stamina to increase, the weights slowly have to get heavier as you adjust to them, which means leaving your comfort zone. If you are great at organic, grounded sound design using minimal processing, try designing something more "sci-fi" using only synths. Love making 8-bit music? Challenge yourself to write a full orchestral piece.

If you're worried about finding the time to add extra creative challenges to your practice routine then don't worry, because I have a simple sound design exercise that can be done anywhere, anytime - whether you're in line at the grocery store, sitting in traffic or going for a walk. I call it 'field analysis', and it goes like this:

- Observe! What can you see? What can you hear?
- Analyse! Why can you hear it? How is the sound being produced? What are the mechanical processes involved in producing the sound?
- Apply! How could these sounds work in a game? What processes could you use to make something cool?

If you're a composer, try looking out for sounds that would make for cool DIY instruments, and try to come up with a motif for an imaginary scene in a game or a soundtrack to what you're experiencing at that moment.

- Observe! What can you see? What can you hear?
- Analyse! What kind of musical application could that sound have? How would you go about recording and sampling it?
- Apply! How might a piece of music use that sample sound? What kind of emotion would that music convey?

These are just two examples, but you could think about how you'd implement a sound, how you'd process a sound to reflect the environment it's in, anything – and if you find yourself with a cool idea, then the ball's rolling, and it's time to get creative!

GETTING UNSTUCK

Occasionally, we will encounter a creative problem that we can't seem to find a solution to. When this happens, we can use a different 'creative lens' to reframe the problem and examine it from another perspective. Just like how optical lenses can magnify or reduce an image, or change the way we perceive different colours, creative lenses can allow us to focus on different aspects of a problem, and help us identify solutions. This can mean finding novel uses for props and samples – a leather belt becomes a creaking rope, a noisy radiator becomes an ancient spaceship, etc. – but it can also mean viewing things from the perspective of a different discipline.

Whenever I spend a significant amount of time focused on a specific audio 'food group', I become hyper-focused on the context in which it's applied. For example, when I'm creating ambiences, my ears become attuned to the minute details within sounds – leaves dancing in the wind and how they sound as they brush across different surfaces. Alternatively, when I'm involved in a lot of Foley production, I'll start to fixate on the sounds I make as I move and interact with my environment – paper rustling, keys jangling, and so on. If I ever feel stuck on a task, I try switching lenses and seeing if another perspective offers me any potential answers. Here are a few methods I like to use that you can try for yourself:

Go Analog

An easy way to change perspectives is simply to step away from the screen! Try brainstorming ideas using a pen and paper, describing the sounds you want to make or sketching out a prototype for an audio tool you want to build. The lack of external input gives you the space to think for yourself, draw little illustrations and iterate quickly. Don't be afraid to make a mess – you'll be translating your ideas onto the computer in the end; whatever gets you to the answer in the meantime is valid.

Take a Break

It's easy to lose sight of the bigger picture when we get stuck on something. Sometimes, the best thing to do is step away and take a break - with some distance, it can be easier to see the forest for the trees and determine where to invest your energy in order to move forward. I have two preferred methods for this: First is simply going for a walk somewhere nice - no headphones, phone on silent, just being among nature for a while. The second method is to play the game I'm working on in "end-user mode," playing a compiled version of the build on a TV rather than through the editor on my computer. If I notice anything related to work, I write it down, but the primary goal is to experience the game from the player's perspective.

Change Your Tools

We tend to use the same plugins, microphones, DAW and other tools over and over because we are most comfortable with them, but by swapping out your regular tools and introducing some discomfort, we can force ourselves to engage with problems in new ways. It might seem counterintuitive when our goal is typically to reduce friction in our workflow, but when we're already struggling with a task, the right bit of extra challenge can sometimes lead to a breakthrough.

Change Your Space

I wrote the majority of this book sitting in my bed, on my laptop – my desk is my workplace, and my bed is my comfy, creative place. However, the biggest breakthroughs were often made in my favourite coffee shop, thinking about chapters that I was struggling with and scribbling on a notepad. Changing your environment can be just as powerful as changing your tools, so don't be afraid to take your work on the road if you're getting stuck.

Make Something, Anything

It's absolutely crazy that we can imagine a sound and then bring it into existence by crafting it out of other sounds that we manipulate, shape and stack. If you're truly stuck, then make something – anything – without judgement or critique, and let the process carry you. It's always harder to write when you're staring at a blank page, so just throw something out there to get the ball rolling.

"What Would Greg Do?"

Asking yourself, "what would x person do?" in tricky situations is a clichéd but effective way to change our lens. Trying to view the world, or simply a creative problem that you're struggling with, through someone else's eyes can be a great way to generate new solutions that you might not have thought of otherwise.

WHAT'S NEXT?

Our last chapter is probably our most important. We'll be talking about the unpleasant spectre in the room: Burnout – why you should take it seriously, and ways you can avoid it and look after yourself.

Balance and Burnout

11

I had always thought that I was immune to burnout – I was passionate and loved what I did, so it couldn't happen, right? I was wrong. You can become burned out from anything, *especially* if it's something that you're passionate about, as that passion starts to become an obsession. It's a difficult thing to deal with and unfortunately a lot more common than people think, particularly in the games industry. Like as things mental health, burnout affects everyone in slightly different ways, but it typically starts small and grows over time, slowly impacting every facet of our lives as it does - **not just our work, but our hobbies and social lives too**. I hadn't realised that burnout is more than just being unable to do your job until it happened to me.

So how do we avoid burnout, and what do we do if we fall victim to it? First, let's look outward and try to understand burnout – what it is, where it comes from, and how to spot the warning signs. Then, we'll look inward and get to know ourselves better in order to understand how it affects us personally and what we can do to avoid it. I hope you like metaphors, because this chapter is nothing but.

THE GARDEN

The way I like to visualise a healthy, balanced life is by imagining a lush garden full of different varieties of plants and wildlife – each one contributes to keeping the ecosystem in balance. In our lives, these represent different activities like:

- Working a fulfilling job.
- Eating regular, healthy meals.
- Exercising regularly.
- Spending time in nature.
- Socialising regularly with friends and family.

DOI: 10.1201/9781003368854-12

- Self-care and hygiene.
- Taking routine breaks to rest and getting quality sleep.
- Hobbies and interests like video games, reading, etc.

However, life is unpredictable and eventful like the weather, and when the weather gets extreme it can tip the balance of elements within the garden. These events can be big or small, good or bad, but they introduce change into our lives and bring some amount of internal and/or external pressure with them. For example:

- A deadline at work or university.
- An opportunity, such as a new client or job.
- A forced lifestyle change from sustaining an injury, having a baby, or being unable to leave your house because of a pandemic.

To alleviate this pressure, we reprioritise tasks to meet the new challenge head-on. In the short term, this is a fine strategy, but in the long term, if the situation doesn't change and the pressure continues to rise, things can start to get dangerous. Our daily lives, which used to be a balance of different activities, become monotonous; the garden that was once colourful and thriving becomes a monoculture, overgrown and dominated by a single species, and the other elements surrounding it begin to suffer:

- Working a ~~fulfilling~~ stressful job.
- Eating ~~regular~~ sporadic, ~~healthy~~ unhealthy meals.
- ~~Exercising regularly.~~
- ~~Spending time in nature.~~
- Socialising ~~regularly~~ rarely with friends and family.
- ~~Self-care and hygiene.~~
- ~~Taking regular breaks to rest and~~ getting ~~quality~~ very little sleep.
- ~~Hobbies and interests like video games, reading etc.~~

The problem with neglecting other activities in favour of a single one like work is that those other activities help us recharge our energy and creativity. This balance is what keeps us healthy, and our health is the most important pillar in our lives. When we remove the things that recharge our energy and start doing more things that drain it, we end each day with a net loss – we are now, slowly, burning out. This process is often subtle – it can happen without us even noticing - but the longer it continues, the worse it gets. We start to feel stretched thin at first, then overwhelmed, and then exhausted. Things we previously enjoyed that restored our energy become a chore. There is a constant underlying feeling of stress, pressure and dread that eats away at us, eventually starting to affect our physical health as our body tries to tell us to stop.

Our mental health also suffers immensely – our emotions become unstable, we become irritable and short-tempered, and previously manageable situations become nearly impossible to cope with. Simply getting out of bed in the morning now requires tremendous willpower and there is never a day you don't feel tired. Continuing down this path eventually leads to full-blown burnout, which can take years to recover from. When this happens, our metaphorical garden has been taken over completely by invasive weeds, and we're left with the huge task of rooting them all out, fertilising the soil and repopulating the garden with new plants.

PASSION AND PRESSURE

Passion and pressure often come as a package deal - when you care about something deeply, you want to do it well, and that expectation creates pressure. When we don't live up to our own expectations, it can feel very personal. "You're a failure, you're not good enough, you don't belong here" – these are all thoughts that have lived in my mind and still occasionally visit me. The fact that you're reading this book right now shows that you are motivated and passionate about game audio, and this is a good thing. This industry attracts people who are incredibly passionate about what they do and often presents barriers to entry that act as a filter separating those who really want to be here from those who don't.

That flame of passion that drives you is important, as it's the thing that helps you push forward when the going gets tough, that motivates you to put yourself out there and attend networking events even when it feels terrifying. I want to work with people who love game audio, who are keen to learn and who are up for a challenge – I want to share in their passion. If you can learn how to control your flame and use its power without exhausting it, you will go far in this industry and the world in general. But fire is dangerous, and when the flames go unchecked it's easy to burn yourself, which is exactly what happened to me.

When Passion Becomes Obsession

Before I had a day job doing game audio, I spent most of my free time practising, learning and developing my skills. Eventually, I got my first job, working with Sean on a startup studio's first game. I was out of my depth at first, having jumped into the role of game designer with no previous experience, and there was a lot of uncertainty about whether the project would receive enough funding to continue, which of course added more pressure. Then the COVID-19 pandemic hit, and it slowly became clear that I would have to find a new job. I started freelancing again, building up my online presence and networking in preparation to find a new job. After I landed my job at Soundcuts, I continued to make YouTube videos in my free time, and began to develop a strong passion for the education side of game audio. The more videos I uploaded, the more messages and emails I got asking for advice on how to get into game audio. I was spending a lot of time replying and sharing links to different learning resources, so I collected all of the best ones onto a spreadsheet, which I shared online. It got a great response, but the emails kept coming. One day, I decided to sit down and write the framework for a course that would teach you all the things you needed to get a job in game audio.

I'm a very ambitious person, which can be a double-edged sword. I set out to do things that others would write off as crazy, and sometimes I achieve them. Just as often, however, I bite off more than I can chew but keep going anyway, convinced that it'll all work out in the end. As I planned out the course, the scope grew bigger and bigger until it became clear that I wouldn't be able to cover everything. That was okay, though – there was already a lot of amazing information out there; it just needed to be simplified and compiled into a course format that people could follow easily. That's when the idea for *Game Audio Learning* began to take shape. Instead of a course, it would be a website, freely available to everyone. I worked on it in my spare time for an entire year, all the while continuing to make YouTube videos and working my day job. When it finally launched, I felt like I had run a marathon to get it over the finish line.

After a marathon, it's important to let your body rest and recover, but instead, I continued running and even picked up the pace as new opportunities started to come my way. I said yes to everything because it all sounded exciting and I was afraid that if I didn't take an opportunity, I'd regret it later. I was now in a full sprint, but there was no longer a clear finish line, and my pace kept increasing. Each new project required more of my time and attention, and soon, I found myself spending the majority of my day in front of the computer, working on various game audio-related projects. No matter how much work I did, my to-do list only seemed to grow. The bigger it got, the more stressed I became, and as the pressure mounted, I started feeling guilty whenever I wasn't being 'productive' and working on something.

It became really hard to relax, and I stopped doing a lot of the things that had previously brought me joy or helped me recharge, like going climbing, cooking good meals, and spending time with friends. I started to lose motivation for my job, because I was so distracted by all the tasks that I had to do before and after that I seldom felt like I had completed a good day's work. There I was, teaching people how to get into the game audio industry, actively burning out and losing my own passion for it. I had stopped pursuing most of my hobbies; my identity had become completely tied to game audio and the projects I'd taken on. When I eventually met up with a friend who worked outside of the industry – and who barely understood what I actually did for a living – the bubble finally burst, and I realised that I had no life. I had become so wrapped up in game audio that I had lost all perspective and forgotten about the world outside of my job. Things had to change. If I kept going like this, I would end up destroying my passion, my career and my health – I needed to get my life back.

Identity and Passion

You are not your work.

Jamie Lee

In a creative field like game audio, it's common for our work to be a large part of our identity and self-perception. This isn't an inherently unhealthy thing – when we are intrinsically motivated to do something because we experience joy from it, we refer to that as *harmonious passion*.[1] This type of passion comes *from* our identity – because we *are* creative – and is why we feel a connection to our work. We love what we do, but know when to stop and focus on other things in our lives.

In the story above, my passion was harmonious at first, but as I invested more and more time into game audio and started neglecting other parts of my life, it turned into an *obsessive passion*. This kind of passion is parasitic, slowly taking over our entire lives – it is the invasive weed that destroys our garden. Instead of being intrinsically motivated to do something because we love it, we are primarily *extrinsically* motivated, doing things because we feel like we have to *for* our identity – "Without my work, what am I?"

The danger of obsessive passion is that our self-worth becomes deeply connected to our (perceived) productivity, output and skill level. This leads us to endlessly compare ourselves to others and often feel like we're not good enough, nor doing enough. This is a feedback loop that goes round and round as the pressure mounts and the guilt rises. We do more to cope, increasing our workload until it consumes us entirely. The lesson is simple: Have a life, pursue your hobbies and spend time with friends and family.

Work to live, rather than live to work.

Jon Kelliher

It sounds simple when put like that, but in reality, our lives aren't flat lines – things are forever happening that push and pull on us, making a perfect work-life balance near-impossible to achieve. Instead of striving for a perfect balance – which is unrealistic and unattainable – think of life as a journey through ever-changing seasons. Each season has a different climate and weather, allowing different plants to grow and prosper in our garden. We change our priorities and shift focus as the seasons change, dedicating our time to preparing a job application, putting work and hobbies aside when having a baby, or putting more time into a hobby when we feel like we need to focus on ourselves and rest/recharge.

Crunch

In game development, the workload fluctuates frequently, ramping up before a major milestone and then dropping off for a while after. Pushing harder for brief periods of time is normal in the run-up to a deadline, but when the pressure stays up with no end in sight, we're in danger of burning ourselves out. You've probably heard the term "Crunch" used to describe these extended periods of high workloads, which are one of the main causes of burnout (Figure 11.1).[2]

Crunch is, sadly, a fairly common problem in the games industry. Video games are incredibly complicated things to make, requiring people from so many different disciplines to collaborate and coordinate. On top of that, the tools and technology used to make games are often being developed at the same time as the games themselves, making technical hiccups almost inevitable. These factors make it difficult to plan and budget accurately, leading to deadlines that aren't as generous as they initially seemed when the workload

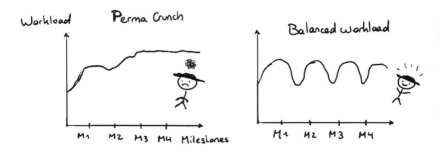

FIGURE 11.1   The energy you expend to work has to come from somewhere; A healthy project ensures you have enough downtime to recover that energy.

increases but the budget doesn't – if the deadline can't or won't be moved, we end up crunching to get the project out the door. Being the last discipline in the development pipeline, audio folks are at particular risk of having to crunch to compensate for delays that happened in earlier processes – this is why it's so important to communicate with other departments to avoid being blindsided by sudden delays or increases in workload.

Of course, crunch isn't unique to AAA projects with large teams – it can happen just as easily when working on a small indie title with a handful of people. There are many stories of employers forcing their staff to crunch, but in my own experience, the pressure is often social and unintentional – seeing your colleagues working late makes you want to join them. We don't want to let our team down by not pulling our weight, and our passion for what we do drives us to overwork ourselves. Ultimately, we all want to release a game that we can be proud of, and when we don't have enough time to make that happen, we have to either give up our own time or accept that the game won't be finished by the deadline, which may or may not be an option. As I mentioned above, the workload in game development is like a sine curve, and it's normal to have to put in a few extra hours here and there when a milestone is looming, but if days of overwork turn into weeks and months, we need to make a change before it's too late.

HOW NOT TO BURN OUT

The circumstances that lead us to need to crunch are typically pipeline problems beyond our control as individuals. If you're faced with frequent periods of crunch, the best course of action may be simply to look for a job elsewhere, at a studio with a healthier work culture. That said, there are things we can control, and can do to help protect ourselves, fortifying our garden against invasive plants. Being honest with ourselves is a common theme in this next section – sometimes it can be uncomfortable to acknowledge how we feel and why, but our wellbeing is the single most important thing in our lives, so we owe it to ourselves to try as best we can.

Fences – Limits and Boundaries

Boundaries are our first line of defence against crunch and burnout – they're the fence keeping your garden safe from unwanted intruders by ensuring that we always have enough time and energy for ourselves. This can mean learning to say no to unreasonable requests, or when we don't have time for more work. Turning down opportunities can be hard, especially when we're just starting out and hungry for experience, but there will always be more, so don't pressure yourself (or let anyone pressure you) into accepting a bad deal or taking on more than you can manage at once.

Boundaries can also mean simply leaving the office on time and communicating our needs to our co-workers or boss. Thanks to smartphones, we're able to carry our work around with us at all times, so turn off work-related notifications outside of work hours to avoid being interrupted while you're trying to relax. It's not poor communication to be unavailable outside of your work hours – that Teams/Slack message can wait until tomorrow. It may be tempting to go the extra mile when you first start a new job, but reputations have to be built over time, and overworking for that long will see you burn out (as well as building a reputation as "the person who overworks," which will do you no favours). Most importantly, tell your lead/boss how you're getting on and what you're thinking, good and bad. If you're enjoying something, let them know; if you're struggling with something, let them know! It's their responsibility to look after you, but they can only do so if you tell them how you feel.

Working From Home

The boundaries that separate our work and home lives are especially important – and difficult to enforce – when we work from home. As we covered in Chapter 8, one useful strategy is to have a separate space exclusively for working. If you don't have a spare room available to use as an office, you can use a screen door or curtains to create a physical separation between your workspace and your living space during the day.

If you use your own computer for work, create two user accounts on it – one for working, and one for personal use or alternatively a second desktop to switch between – and if you're a freelancer, have dedicated email and social media accounts for business matters. Remember that 'going home on time' still applies when working from home. Set alarms for scheduled breaks, lunchtime, and the end of the day, and stick to them – log out of your work account, and don't allow yourself to keep going late into the evening.

Plant Selection and Spacing – Focus

When designing a garden, we have to choose plants that are suited to the environment and ensure that there's space for them to grow and flourish – not all plants can survive in all gardens, and nothing will grow well if the garden is overcrowded.

Make sure the activities, commitments and responsibilities you take on align with your priorities, and make an effort to learn and recognise your limits, to avoid taking on more than you can handle, or things that you aren't yet ready for.

Weeding – Removing Negative Influences

An important part of gardening is removing dead branches and unwanted plants. Similarly, we have to look after ourselves by identifying and cutting out any activities, relationships, or habits that are draining our energy and impacting our wellbeing. It's not an easy thing to do, especially if it means cutting toxic people out of your life, but it's worth it in the long run. Don't be overzealous, of course – there's a balance to be struck between looking after yourself and being callous – but where you can, removing negative influences creates space for positivity and growth.

Nourishing Your Soil – Self-Care

Just as healthy soil is essential for plants to grow, taking care of your physical and mental health will enable you to deliver great work and avoid burning out. Acknowledging our emotions and knowing where our limits are is a key part of this process, helping us learn to recognise when we're pushing ourselves and need to slow down. Don't try to fight or suppress feelings of stress or tiredness, but accept them without judging yourself and address them proactively, be that by seeking support from friends, practising self-care, or seeing a professional therapist. There is absolutely no shame in going to therapy. My mother was a therapist, a lot of my friends have been to therapy in the past, and so have I. Understanding ourselves is key to living a happier and healthier life, so learn to identify the warning signs and take steps to keep yourself well.

Enjoying the Fruits of Your Labour – Gratitude

Ultimately, tending to your garden is not just about the work, but also enjoying and appreciating the rewards it brings. Savouring the view and tasting the fruit from the trees reminds us why we do this in the first place. Celebrate victories, be proud of what you've accomplished and how much you've grown – being grateful for the things we have is one of the best things we can do to improve our wellbeing. Taking the time to appreciate even a small victory is a good way to practise that gratitude, be that a simple acknowledgement written in a journal, or a tangible reward like treating yourself to a nice meal.

Putting in the Work

Tending to your garden isn't a one-off activity – it's a constant process, forcing us to adapt as the garden grows and its needs change with the seasons. Like a garden, our wellbeing requires ongoing care and attention. Check in with yourself from time to time; be honest about your needs, and be proactive in taking steps to maintain a healthy lifestyle and prevent burnout. I find journalling to be a great way to both ask myself these important questions and keep track of my answers over time.

Being able to reflect back on previous answers also helps me to identify patterns, good or bad, and work to reinforce or challenge them respectively. Try using the following questions as starting points for your reflection:

- How am I feeling right now about my life, inside and outside of work?
- What are the things that are important to me currently?
- Do I feel able to focus on the things that are important to me?
- What things, if any, are putting me under pressure?
- Do I feel able to manage this pressure?
- What are my current goals, in the short and long term?
- What can I do to move towards my goals?

GO OUTSIDE

For all of the ideas we've covered in this chapter, the best way to combat burnout is to spend time away from work and the industry altogether. Do things in your downtime that aren't related to game audio, and away from screens completely if possible. If you don't leave the house to go to work, you need to make doubly sure that you get out regularly. Build things like grocery shopping or going to the gym into your normal routine to ensure that you get some fresh air and exercise. Make time to socialise and hang out with people, ideally in person, and have a support network around you that can check in and make sure you're looking after yourself. Have friends outside of the industry – people who aren't into game audio or even video games full stop, they will help ground you. Video games are great, but the world outside of games is pretty good too, and a life full of contrast and variety will allow you to enjoy your time spent gaming even more.

WHAT'S NEXT?

We're almost at the end of our time together, but before then, I have one last piece of advice for you...

REFERENCES

1. Vallerand, R.J. *et al.* (2003) 'Les passions de l'ame: on obsessive and harmonious passion', *Journal of Personality and Social Psychology*, 85(4), pp. 756–67. doi: https://doi.org/10.1037/0022-3514.85.4.756
2. Take This (2016) *Crunch Hurts: How Unmitigated Overwork Harms Employee Health, Productivity, and Your Studio's Bottom Line.* Available at: https://www.takethis.org/2016/08/crunch-hurts-white-paper/ (Accessed: 09 January 2024).

Outro
Before You Go…

Congratulations, you've made it to the end of the *Pocket Mentor for Game Audio*! We've covered a lot of topics throughout this book, and I hope you've learned something valuable from your time reading it. If there is one thing in particular that I hope you take away from this book, however, it's that you have *potential*. The capacity to grow and improve is exactly what employers want to see from someone entering this industry – your job is to showcase that potential and make it clear that you're willing to push yourself in order to achieve it.

I like to consider this as a person's "trajectory" – based on their current actions, are they setting themselves up to reach their full potential? Time alone won't see you grow and improve unless you put in the legwork, through networking, practising your skills and continuous learning. Making active efforts to grow and improve increases the chances of the people around you recognising what you're capable of, and the likelihood that you'll achieve it, too. Had a successful job or networking event recently? Don't kill your momentum, keep making forward strides and building on that success (Figure O.1).

Everything we've covered in this book, from finding ways to make learning easier, to being a team player, to improving your workflow, has been in service of building and maintaining that forward momentum. During the writing process, I read a number of excellent books all about productivity and motivation (you've probably noticed that it's something I'm passionate about!). Of those, there were five that stood out to me in particular – if this book has piqued your interest, then I can highly recommend the following as further reading:

- *Diary of a CEO* by Steven Bartlett.
- *Essentialism* by Greg McKeown.
- *The Crux* by Richard Rumelt.
- *Steal Like An Artist* by Austin Kleon.
- *Upstream* by Dan Heath.

DOI: 10.1201/9781003368854-13

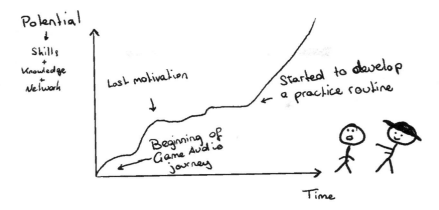

FIGURE O.1   Trajectory = (skills + knowledge + network) * time.

Of course, it's important to strike a balance between maintaining an upward trajectory and giving yourself time to rest. Like we covered in the last chapter, no amount of progress is worth paying for with your physical and mental health; balancing progress in your career with a healthy and fulfilled personal life is key. There will be setbacks, moments where you feel like you've ground to a halt and can't get going again, and in those moments it's vital that you give yourself the time to rest and recover. Life is made up of seasons; sometimes you're sprinting and other times you need to walk slowly. I hope you're fortunate enough not to experience burnout for yourself, and that some of the ideas we discussed prove helpful to you in finding your ideal work-life balance.

Finally, don't be a stranger! One of the best things about working in game audio is how welcoming the community is – come find us on Airwiggles and join in the fun. At the end of the day, we're a bunch of nerds with a passion for audio, and being able to share that enthusiasm with others is one of the best parts of the job! And of course, if you're looking for ways to improve or maintain your technical skills, stop by the *GAL* website and check out the content and courses we have available.

I wish you the best of luck on your journey into the world of game audio – I'll see you out there!

Glossary

AAA: A term used to describe game development studios and their projects, typically those that are largest in terms of staff, budget, and/or scope.

Audio Direction: A collection of ideas or constraints used to determine a game's overall sonic aesthetic, and ensure that all of the sounds in the game work together to form a cohesive whole.

Audio Test: An assessment often given to job applicants in game audio to determine their sound design skills.

"Cine" Sounds: Non-diegetic sounds added to create and amplify specific emotions or reinforce what's happening on-screen.

Crunch: A term for periods of extended overtime, relatively common in the last few weeks before a major deadline.

DAW: Digital Audio Workstation, the primary software used to record and edit sounds. The most popular DAWs in the games industry are *Pro Tools* and *Reaper*.

Demo Reel: A short video made up of clips featuring a person's sound design and/or music to showcase their style and abilities.

Foley: A discipline within sound design that focuses on characters' interactions, named after pioneering sound effects artist Jack Foley. Foley artists will often "perform" sound effects such as footsteps or fabric rustling live, synchronising with video manually.

Freelancing: A form of self-employment in which a person takes one-off jobs from various clients, rather than being continuously employed on a single company's payroll.

Frequency Spectrum: The range of human hearing, approximately from 20Hz to 20kHz.

Game Design: The process of designing how a game works on a mechanical level, the systems involved, and how (or why) the player will interact with them.

Game Engine: Software in which a game is "built," where all of the assets and code are compiled to create the finished product.

Game Jam: A community-driven event in which small teams – made up of hobbyists and professionals alike – build a game or game demo over a few days to a week. Games made at these events are often made available to play for free after the fact.

GDC: The Game Developers Conference, an annual event featuring numerous presentations from industry figures across all manner of disciplines.

Implementation: The process of putting audio assets into a game, controlling when and how they play back.

Indie: A term used to describe game development studios and projects that are smaller in terms of staff, budget and/or scope.

Localisation: The process of translating a title into different languages, including written and audio dialogue, as well as menu text.

Middleware: Software used for the implementation, debugging and mixing of audio. Middleware can be used to control in-game audio in real time, for the creation of interactive scores.

NDA: Non-disclosure agreement, a contract that specifies information that cannot be shared with third parties. In game development, this usually means being unable to share information about unannounced projects with people who aren't directly involved.

Outboard Gear: Pieces of dedicated processing hardware external to the user's main computer. Audio has to be sent from the main computer to the external gear and back again, or from the microphone to the computer via the outboard gear during recording.

Pipeline: A term for a macro-level process or discipline, such as "Dialogue" or "Foley". Pipelines are made up of many smaller processes and logistical stages.

Plugin: A piece of software that can be used as an add-on to another program, such as an audio effect in a DAW or a scripting tool in a game engine.

Publisher: A company that handles the processes involved in releasing a game on behalf of the developer, including marketing, press releases and the production of physical media (if the game is to have a physical release). Publishers can also serve as the primary source of funding for a project.

QA Testing: Playing a game (usually an in-progress development build) with the aim of finding bugs and technical issues that can be reproduced and passed on to the developers to be fixed.

Scripting: Low-level programming that controls the playback of audio in a game. Different engines handle scripting in different ways, from node-based systems to traditional lines of code.

Shipped Title: A game that has been completed and made available to the public.

Stereo Field: The space between the left and right channels in a stereo pair. Sounds can be "placed" in the stereo field by balancing the volume of the sound in the left and right channels, or moved through the field by adjusting the balance over time.

Technical Sound Design: A specialism within sound design with a focus on implementation.

Transient: The initial "attack" phase of a sound, identifiable as the brief, loud noise at the start of a waveform.

VFX: Visual Effects, an area of game development responsible for creating and implementing visuals such as explosions, water, and particle effects.

Printed in the United States
by Baker & Taylor Publisher Services